About ISTE

The International Society for Technology in Education (ISTE) is the trusted source for professional development, knowledge generation, advocacy, and leadership for innovation. ISTE is the premier membership association for educators and education leaders engaged in improving teaching and learning by advancing the effective use of technology in PK–12 and teacher education.

Home of the National Educational Technology Standards (NETS) and ISTE's annual conference and exposition (formerly known as NECC), ISTE represents more than 100,000 professionals worldwide. We support our members with information, networking opportunities, and guidance as they face the challenge of transforming education. To find out more about these and other ISTE initiatives, visit our website at **www.iste.org**.

As part of our mission, ISTE Book Publishing works with experienced educators to develop and produce practical resources for classroom teachers, teacher educators, and technology leaders. Every manuscript we select for publication is carefully peer-reviewed and professionally edited. We value your feedback on this book and other ISTE products. E-mail us at **books@iste.org**.

About the Author

Midge Frazel, MEd

Absorbing the stories around her was made easy for Midge because she is an only child and grandchild. When she purchased her first computer in the early 1980s, she never dreamed that it would become such a large part of her future. Riding the adventure of emerging technology is a digital story of its own; the twists and turns, successes and failures, as well as the communication with people met along the way, have enriched her writing, teaching, and life in ways she had not thought possible a mere twenty years ago.

Guided by the simple philosophy that any teacher can master using the computer in the classroom, Midge is well known for her "low-fat, low-stress," enthusiastic teaching style in professional development workshops for teachers in southeastern Massachusetts. She has authored or co-authored books and articles geared toward classroom teachers, specialists, administrators, and librarians. She maintains a website and a blog on educational technology and is a regular contributor to the educational community Tapped In (www.tappedin.org).

She recently completed her master's degree from Lesley University, all online, of course, at the age of nearly 60. This is a milestone book: the tenth in ten years.

As an adult educator, she was once a medical technologist in two teaching hospitals and ran her own consulting business. Looking to the future, Midge mixes her passion for family history and genealogy into her research by gathering stories of her ancestors along the way.

Acknowledgments

I'd like to thank the people from ISTE who encouraged me to write this book and gave me plenty of time to accomplish the goal. Listening to my endless stream of questions could not have been easy! Fellow author Bard Williams shared his advice and encouragement, as did Kathy Schrock, who was never too busy to answer my questions or listen to my ideas. Thanks also to Ragen Tiliakos for letting me brag that she is my most successful student. (She is.)

Asking people of the educational technology community to contribute and give permission is never easy, and thanking them for it is imperative. Not one person turned me down. My family deserves thanks for all the years I have been teaching and writing. I live every day grateful for the support of my husband Steve, and my daughter Heather and son-in-law Chuck.

Contents

Part I   Telling Stories and Technology   7

Contents

Contents

Introduction

Storytelling is an ancient art, as ancient as the story images drawn on cave walls or the age-old traditions of the oral storyteller. But like all arts, storytelling is finding new means of expression in the modern era. Digital storytelling brings new life to the ancient craft of written or oral storytelling through computer-generated text and multimedia content. In this book you'll discover how K–12 students can blend text, music, images, sounds, and audio narration to produce, in video format, the digital story. You'll see how, through digital story, the audience for student work is expanded to include a local community of peers and family, or even the world beyond.

I will show you how to transform storytelling into digital storytelling by incorporating computer-based, multimedia elements and by using the computer to show and tell the story. This electronic medium is one your students understand and feel connected to. Digital stories are visual, using photographs or scanned artwork. Digital stories are auditory, using voice narration that can provide students valuable experience with using their own speaking voice. Music and sound effects can be woven into the story to add emotional depth to the presentation. We'll examine how in the chapters of this book.

You don't need to be an expert in teaching writing to use digital storytelling in your classroom. Digital storytelling is applicable across the curriculum, at all grade levels, and for the distributed learning population in every school. Whether you are a novice or a seasoned technologist, you'll discover that there are many excellent websites to help you learn these skills and to provide related resources, much of it available at no charge as Web 2.0 content. And, with the array of digital resources accessible via the World Wide Web, you, the classroom teacher, have many options concerning which combination of media will meet your specific curriculum objectives.

When you picked up this book, you may have been wondering: What is digital storytelling? Why should I use it in my classroom? Digital storytelling can be many things to many different teachers and many different students. Here are some of the things digital storytelling can accomplish in your classroom:

- Digital storytelling engages students and can help motivate them to learn core curriculum content.

- Digital storytelling addresses the need for relevancy in learning for today's K–12 students.

- Digital storytelling provides a hands-on, active instructional format, helping educators meet the needs of diverse student groups.

- Digital storytelling promotes group activities in the classroom.

- Digital storytelling can be individualized within the context of a class assignment.

- Digital storytelling provides students with opportunities to apply emerging technologies as part of their learning.

- Digital storytelling can support team teaching and learning across the curriculum.

In this book, I will show you how each of these elements might apply to your classroom and your instruction. I'll also show you how digital storytelling can be applied in a variety of creative circumstances. I'll demonstrate ways you can apply digital storytelling in your classroom, or as a way to link your classroom to the world beyond. I'll also show you how educators are using digital storytelling to work within the framework of emerging technologies by applying these tools in their own day-to-day work.

This book has been designed to provide resources, ideas, and guidelines for the use of digital tools to create, produce, and deliver story and other content through an electronic medium. It is written for all educators and lifelong learners interested in accessing resources for the production of several genres of digital storytelling. I specifically include in this group classroom teachers, K–12 school administrators, curriculum developers, and teacher trainers. In writing the book, I address the teacher in all of you.

How to Use This Book

Make use of this book to design and implement instruction in any K–12 classroom, or to express your own creative urges. I recommend that every teacher who will employ digital storytelling in their instruction create at least one digital story of their own before using the technology with students. You can use this book to guide your own professional development in the process.

Part I provides an overview of digital storytelling, describing in step-by-step detail how to create a digital story through three stages of development: preparation, production, and presentation. We'll examine several genres of digital storytelling and provide examples of assessment rubrics for all three stages. The end product can be a video or audio file, which can be saved on the computer, copied to disc, or posted on file-sharing websites.

The projects we will look at in the context of this book, both collaborative and individual in nature, can also offer students a new perspective on how movies and television shows are produced.

Part II discusses how you can use digital storytelling to build your students' enthusiasm for learning. It provides further examples of ways to use digital storytelling in the classroom and as a bridge to an expanded educational community. Appendix A discusses how teachers can use digital storytelling for their own career and professional development.

You'll find every chapter filled with resources that will expand your awareness of and application of digital storytelling in the classroom. The resources offered in this book include implementation ideas, related websites, instructional tips, and access to professionals in the field. You'll find suggested resources and their sources woven throughout the book, presented in the text, in sidebars, and in Resources listings at the end of each chapter.

Open-ended questions at the end of some of the chapters provide classroom teachers with suggested topics for pre- or post-project class discussion.

PART I

Telling Stories and Technology

There's a story inside each one of us. Storytelling is a natural component of society and culture. Story is based in language and delivered by the tools of the day. The tool may once have been a rock used to etch pictures onto another rock; it may have been a quill or a fountain pen, a printing press, a television screen, or a movie reel. Each generation of every culture has taken advantage of the tools available to them and has developed their own methods of storytelling, and their own ways to present those stories.

For students today, digital tools open a world of creativity and expression that is unique and ever-broadening. Students can reach a wider audience than ever before. The ease of access to these technologies presents new challenges and expanding opportunities for K–12 students and teachers.

Storytelling is always about story, but in this book we present technology and instructional resources to support the use of digital technology to tell and present the story. We'll also address some of the issues connected to accessing intellectual and visual property for publication by reviewing current copyright laws and guidelines.

Introduction to Digital Storytelling

What Is Digital Storytelling?

Digital storytelling is a process that blends media to enrich and enhance the written or spoken word. Leaders in the field have called digital storytelling a new twist to storytelling—multimedia tales are the modern expression of an ancient art. Digital storytelling can encompass many topics beyond the classic story, take many forms, and employ an ever-expanding array of software applications. A digital story may have a narration overlay and sometimes a music background; it may combine, in any number of ways, images, audio, and video to tell a story or to make a factual presentation. In many cases, sound, music, and images surround the written or narrated content.

Because of the limits on storage capacity for video on most school networks, digital stories must be kept short in length. Generally, websites that store finished digital stories for viewing and sharing also have size limits. But, although shorter than the classic oral presentation, a digital story can make up in content what it foregoes in length. Digital stories are most often transferred into an 8- to 10-minute video so that they can be viewed over and over. They can be stored online and shared from a distance with an anytime, anyplace audience.

The presentation element of the digital story is an essential component of the process and the product. The construction of reliable standards-based content is another important component that educators will address within the parameters of their own areas of qualification. This book provides assessment standards and rubrics for the application of the technology and encourages educators to overlay and employ the state and national standards appropriate and applicable for their subject areas.

Why Digital Storytelling?

To a classroom teacher, time is more precious than gold. If you could have one wish, it would probably be for more time. Where will you find the time to develop a digital storytelling project with your students? And more importantly, why should you?

Many of today's students already use these creative and collaborative technologies during their own time. Most view them as key components of the world they live in and the world they will one day work in. They will need these skills in college and in the workplace. Furthermore, they are more likely to engage in the work of telling a story when the result will be presented as a multimedia activity. This is their world.

They are already telling their stories on YouTube and Facebook and any number of Web 2.0 content or social networking sites. As educators, we can use the emerging technologies to our advantage to foster learning, creativity, and enthusiasm.

The technology to produce professional-quality work is now accessible to students. Digital story creation has the potential to motivate and engage students, and to demonstrate to them the complexity of project management and the importance of audience. These activities help them develop and hone skill sets they may need in their future workplaces. Digital storytelling, in its numerous forms and genres, is a good fit for today's classrooms. It is well worth the extra effort to learn it and incorporate it into your teaching.

Value of Digital Stories

- Active, not passive, process
- Creates atmosphere of excitement and fun
- Fosters appropriate use of technology within curriculum
- Bridges school and community
- Weaves into all subject areas
- Effective for both visual and auditory learners

How Does Digital Storytelling Fit in Your Classroom?

It is important to understand that digital storytelling is not only for the language arts classroom. Digital storytelling spans the curriculum, allowing students to see new connections for themselves and uncover new ideas as they assemble resources for their projects. When students write for an audience other than the teacher, they can learn to see writing not as a classroom task done only for its own sake, but as a tool for which they will find many uses in their lives. Visual storytelling can be woven into all subject disciplines. It is also a good way to engage visual and auditory learners in writing.

Websites such as the Writing Site (www.thewritingsite.org/resources/curriculum/) provide ideas and links for ways in which digital technology can enhance and support student learning through writing in all content areas. A number of these sites are listed in the Resources section at the end of this chapter.

Digital storytelling also fits into a variety of teaching methodologies. Project-based learning lends itself to digital storytelling. The hands-on, individualized nature of the process makes it suitable in the framework of Garner's multiple intelligences theory for a cross-section of curriculum-based projects. When English Language Learner (ELL) students are integrated in a regular classroom, digital storytelling projects support differentiated learning environments and can even assist the teacher, who can provide individually paced project-based learning. Many teachers I have talked with and worked with have also successfully employed classroom teams as part of the digital storytelling process.

Here are a few examples of ideas for matching tasks with multiple intelligences one teacher uses in her digital storytelling planning for a unit on weather:

- Linguistic: brainstorm and develop the text of the story

- Spatial: decide on photographs and movies (visuals)

- Body-Kinesthetic: decide and teach presentation of the story; create movie

- Musical: create music, sound effects, and set mood of the story

- Naturalistic: study and report on the effects of weather for the story

- Interpersonal: work with the story map and the presentation

- Intrapersonal: develop the self-refection section of the story (emotional)

- Spatial: decide on photographs and movies (visuals)

- Mathematical-Logical: project time management— length of story and slide timings

> Middle school students learn best when they are actively engaged with the content. When students participate in hands-on, inquiry-based learning, they develop lasting skills that often translate into higher levels of student achievement. Lessons that include technology applications provide teachers with ways to motivate students into becoming active, real-world learners.
>
> *Teaching Today*
> *(http://tinyurl.com/a2nvmg/)*

Not every curriculum benchmark can be met with digital storytelling. Applying digital storytelling depends on individual classroom and curriculum goals, grade level, content, timing, available resources, administrative support, and so on. Consider your circumstances carefully before embarking on digital storytelling in your classroom.

Educators' Podcasts on Digital Storytelling

Several nationally known educators have published podcasts about digital storytelling. Some have been working directly with teachers and their students to develop digital storytelling projects. They share with their listening audience the powerful experience that digital storytelling is bringing to classrooms everywhere. You don't need a digital audio player, such as an iPod, to listen to the audio programs. They will play on your computer in the free, downloadable iTunes software.

Tim Wilson, "The Savvy Technologist"

Blog: www.technosavvy.org

Subscribe at iTunes by searching for "Savvy Technologist"

Feed: feeds.feedburner.com/technosavvy/podcast

Podcast: Joe Lambert: Digital Storytelling Part 1

Podcast: Bernajean Porter: Digital Storytelling Part 2 and Part 3

Wesley Fryer, "Moving at the Speed of Creativity"

Blog: www.speedofcreativity.org

Subscribe at iTunes by searching for "Wesley Fryer"

Feed: feeds.feedburner.com/speedofcreativity/podcasts

Podcast 184: Online Digital storytelling Curriculum from Independent Student Media

Podcast 188: The Oklahoma Digital Centennial Project

Pioneers in Digital Storytelling

Bernajean Porter and Joe Lambert have been called the queen and king of digital storytelling. They earned these titles as recognition for their early contributions to the field. Both have authored books and provide extensive resources on their respective websites, DigiTales: The Art of Telling Digital Stories (www.digitales.us) and the Center for Digital Storytelling (www.storycenter.org). Their sites are well worth your time.

Two other leading experts in digital storytelling are Gail Matthews-DeNatale of Simmons College in Boston, Massachusetts (see page 150), and Carole McCulloch of the Digital Storytelling Network in Baranduda, Victoria, Australia. They work with educators to help them learn both the "digital" and the "story" elements of digital storytelling.

As the leader of the Digital Storytelling Network in her country, Carole shares her story "Digistories Downunder" as a global example of digital storytelling. The figure on the following page shows an example of a digital story she created titled "Mirrors of Life Collage."

Digistories Downunder

By Carole McCulloch

Digital storytelling is an embedded innovative practice amongst educationalists in all sectors of Australia. Teachers in primary, secondary, community, and tertiary institutions have embraced this powerful media for a wide range of purposes in teaching and learning.

Mirrors of Life collage from McCulloch's Digistories Downunder

Primary school teachers are implementing the digital storytelling process as digital literacy development for learners as young as 7 and are enabling the achievements of their 12-year-old graduate students to be displayed using digital story formats—providing an audio/visual e-portfolio for themselves, their parents, and teachers.

Students in upper grades of primary school are teaching the elders in local retirement villages how to create and distribute their life stories using the digital storytelling methodology. This has provided a very special bond between the young and the elderly in community environments, never before envisioned. Some of these stories have been uploaded to websites, saved on CDs and DVDs, and now provide yet another very powerful communication strategy and teaching tool.

Secondary school students are building digital portfolios to document their learning journeys in high schools with digital stories. They are forging new links among one another and their local communities using digital stories to bridge the generational gap. Some students are visiting and photographing local employment environments and using a story narrative to link the images for an introduction into the world of work. Skill shortage areas are being highlighted in local regional towns and the voice of the current generation of students is being heard loudly about their employment prospects through story.

More students have been using digital storytelling to bond and bind together their experiences in "living in the city" projects—growing in their capacity to use ICT and enabling disadvantaged youths to experience such things as Tai Chi in the City Square, looking after their health, investigating jobs and positions, working in teams, developing leadership qualities, and above all sharing their journeys and their stories with their friends and families.

Mature-aged learners, enrolled in a range of tertiary study areas, are trialing the use of digital cameras, mobile phones, and mobile voice recorders to capture and share stories on mobile devices. They have experimented with the display of their stories as short videos in iHubs in capital cities, providing a summary of the attractions and a view of life in the city for tourists and visitors.

Apprentices are using digital storytelling to demonstrate their competencies in a wide range of learning modules such as Automotive, Art and Design, Bakery, Bricklaying, Butchery, Carpentry, and Floristry. They take the digital photos and digital video; they create the narrative and choose the music to accompany it; they develop their own skills in the use of software such as Photo Story, Movie Maker, and Audacity; and they upload their finished movies to a shared drive or MySpace for their tutors.

Whole communities are embracing digital storytelling to capture the rhythm of their regional towns and metropolitan cities, celebrate the achievements of their champions, build a marketing plan for their tourism, and build business plans for small business ownership such as Koori Art and Indigenous Tourism. Collections of these stories are displayed on websites and are sometimes featured in national news media releases.

Networks of digital storytelling enthusiasts, practitioners, and champions have been built, shared, and sustained; networks and communities of practice that provide a rich and multicultural approach to the use of digital stories in education.

Digital storytelling has come full circle in Australia—providing courses for learners of all ages through government-funded projects and through commercial and arts enterprises. Our Australian Digital Storytelling Network has a very strong membership, and digital storytelling champions are actively encouraging and facilitating the uptake of storytelling in a myriad of ways. Teachers have used stories for the disadvantaged, the disabled, and the challenged; and they've used stories to celebrate achievements and leadership.

Recently a funded research project featured the Australian digital storytelling phenomenon as a case study, exploring the multiplicity of complex and engaging strategies for enhancing the engagement of the learners in the learning process.

Digital Story Resources in Australia

Australian digital storytelling:
http://innovateandintegrate.flexiblelearning.net.au

DigiTales wiki: http://digitales.wikispaces.com

Digital Storytelling Network:
www.groups.edna.edu.au/course/view.php?id=107

Ideas for Digital Storytelling

If you are looking for starter ideas for digital storytelling projects, many good examples of completed digital stories on topics such as community, family, identity, and place are available from the website of the Center for Digital Storytelling (www.storycenter.org/stories/).

"Tips for Digital Story Telling" (www.techlearning.com/article/8030/) is a concise and useful article by Jon Orech that covers the entire process from developing a story to presenting the finished product.

Teach Digital: Curriculum by Wesley Fryer (http://teachdigital. pbwiki.com/digitalstorytelling/) is a page listing numerous links to articles on ideas, options, and techniques for digital storytelling. Included are sources for free and royalty-free images, discussions of podcasting and other options for digital storytelling, and tips on getting started in digital storytelling with a limited budget.

"Telling Tales with Technology," by Judy Salpeter (www. techlearning.com/article/3536/), covers the founding and development of the Center for Digital Storytelling. It also includes many examples of digital storytelling as applied in K–12 schools around the country.

Open-Ended Questions for Digital Storytelling

These sample open-ended questions are provided to give you, the educator, ideas for developing critical thinking activities to accompany digital storytelling projects. They are meant as samples, and I encourage you to make up your own to best fit your curriculum and your project. These questions are useful for getting students to think about the parts of their digital story.

- What other ways might this digital story be told?

- What does the music add to the emotion of the digital story?

- What should the audience be able to tell us about your story?

- What additional information might your audience need to understand your story?

- What if we remove the music and the sound effects? Does the story retain its integrity? Why or why not?

Steps in Creating the Digital Story—A Snapshot

The tenets of good writing prevail with digital stories, whether they are told with text or with audio narration. The story or the curriculum content is the most critical part of any digital story. As digital storytelling is applied across the curriculum, teachers should apply the same standards and criteria as with paper-and-pencil writing, research, reflection, and reporting. The primary focus of this text is to assist you, the teacher, in adapting traditional storytelling and other curriculum-based instruction to work with a variety of multimedia digital tools in your classroom.

I have divided the process of digital storytelling into three stages: preparation, production, and presentation. By way of introduction, here is a snapshot of the process.

Preparation Stage

While the story or curriculum-based project is in the preparation stage, it's important to first consider how the piece will be presented because it will affect how the finished story will be produced. During this stage students may develop a concept map, generate storyboards, then create a script for written text or narration. During the preparation process, the teacher should generate a formative assessment rubric (see Chapter 5) to help guide students throughout the process.

Production Stage

Once all the resources and the storyboard are in place, guided by the formative assessment rubric and a partial script, students begin production work. Students select visual and audio elements of the digital story or report. If they are creating a video product they will most likely be working with a slide presentation application. (Video movies may also be an option, but here we will focus on the more widely available technology.) If students are creating a podcast, they will be using audio production software. Guided by storyboard and script, students prepare a narration. The teacher acts as mentor, depending on grade level, and assists with activities such as putting the slides in order or timing the slides. Music and sound effects may be employed. As you will see, all of these elements are available through all kinds of websites and programs. Enthusiastic students create much of their own media.

Note: Throughout the progression of the digital story, the teacher encourages students to consider how the piece will be published or presented.

Working with iMovie from Apple or Microsoft Movie Maker, the slides, images, audio, narration, and any accompanying video are placed into the application's timeline. When the story is completed, it's viewable on the computer screen and saved one final time in its native format. This allows students to go back and edit if needed. Then it is saved as a video file.

Presentation Stage

For presentation, the digital story should be saved onto a file-sharing site or archived onto a CD or DVD. The digital story is played for the classroom or posted to the web.

There are numerous variations of this process and many genres of digital stories and digital storymaking applications. There is classic digital storytelling, and there are photo essays, ePortfolios, and scrapblogs, to name a few. Your students should not be limited by the categories presented here, only by their own imaginations or limitation of tools and time. I will introduce you to a few of the resources available on the Internet.

We will go over, in detail, the process of preparing, producing, and presenting digital stories in Chapters 2, 3, and 4.

Creating the Digital Story

Preparation stage

- Determine audience and how the story will be presented or published

- Create story map, timeline

- Write script

- Prepare narration

- Create formative assessment rubric

Production stage

- Select or create music/sound effects

- Select or create images, video

- Create slides with slide show application

- Apply slide transition special effects

- Render into video file format

- Conduct peer review

- Archive on CD or DVD

Presentation stage

- Play for classroom

- Post to the web

Types of Digital Stories

Digital stories can take many different forms. One example is a digital scrapbook, or e-scrapbook, which extends a traditional scrapbook by preserving materials digitally and allowing students to share their work easily. Scrapblogs are multimedia extensions of traditional scrapbooks.

ePortfolios focus on the learning process. They may be a journal or a photographic record of the student's education experiences, showing growth over time. ePortfolios can demonstrate that the student has mastered the curriculum goals.

Digital photo essays are digital stories created and presented to stimulate learning through auditory (sound) and visual (photographic) elements. Visual literacy, the skill of learning to examine and make sense of visual elements, is important for today's student.

All these formats for digital stories are discussed in greater detail in Chapter 6.

Digital Storytelling with Younger Students

Digital storytelling for young students, in this text, encompasses grade levels under Grade 5. Students of this age have much to say, but they may not have the story-writing skills and the understanding of technology to produce a digital storytelling project. However, their work creating, producing, and presenting digital photo essays and mini-portfolios, with help of the teacher, can be excellent preparation for the creation of curriculum-driven digital storytelling in the middle and high school years.

So don't overlook this age group as you consider digital storytelling. Kidspiration (www.inspiration.com) is a widely known concept mapping tool that can be used with young students who would like to "draw" their own digital story, much as they would with crayons, markers, and paper. Using this application, young students can create a story with simple words, numbers, and concepts. Using a printout, they can tell the story in their own voice while the teacher uses a digital camcorder to record the event. This is an excellent way to introduce students to the concept of audience. Because the accomplishment of the student is highlighted in front of peers, digital storytelling can also promote self-esteem. Digital storytelling can provide young students with their first authorship and presentation experience. Often, for very young students, their topic of choice is autobiographical, a story about themselves, family, and friends—their world.

ISTE Standards and Digital Storytelling

Digital storytelling can help your students meet all of the ISTE National Educational Technology Standards for Students (NETS•S): 1. Creativity and Innovation; 2. Communication and Collaboration; 3. Research and Information Fluency; 4. Critical Thinking, Problem Solving, and Decision Making; 5. Digital Citizenship; and 6. Technology Operations and Concepts (see Appendix B). To help you understand how to connect digital storytelling to the NETS•S, I have included the most applicable ISTE profiles for technology (ICT) literate students, which provide indicators of achievement for different grade/age ranges.

PROFILES

PROFILE FOR TECHNOLOGY (ICT) LITERATE STUDENTS FOR GRADES PK-2

The following experiences with technology and digital resources are examples of learning activities in which students might engage during PK–Grade 2 (ages 4–8):

Illustrate and communicate original ideas and stories using digital tools and media-rich resources. (related NETS•S Standards: 1, 2)

In a collaborative work group, use a variety of technologies to produce a digital presentation or product in a curriculum area. (related NETS•S Standards: 1, 2, 6)

Independently apply digital tools and resources to address a variety of tasks and problems. (related NETS•S Standards: 4, 6)

PROFILE FOR TECHNOLOGY (ICT) LITERATE STUDENTS FOR GRADES 3-5

The following experiences with technology and digital resources are examples of learning activities in which students might engage during Grades 3–5 (ages 8–11):

Produce a media-rich digital story about a significant local event based on first-person interviews. (related NETS•S Standards: 1, 2, 3, 4)

Use digital-imaging technology to modify or create works of art for use in a digital presentation. (related NETS•S Standards: 1, 2, 6)

Conceptualize, guide, and manage individual or group learning projects using digital planning tools with teacher support. (related NETS•S Standards: 4, 6)

PROFILE FOR TECHNOLOGY (ICT) LITERATE STUDENTS FOR GRADES 6–8

The following experiences with technology and digital resources are examples of learning activities in which students might engage during Grades 6–8 (ages 11–14):

Create original animations or videos documenting school, community, or local events. (related NETS•S Standards: 1, 2, 6)

Evaluate digital resources to determine the credibility of the author and publisher and the timeliness and accuracy of the content. (related NETS•S Standard: 3)

Use collaborative electronic authoring tools to explore common curriculum content from the multicultural perspectives with other learners. (related NETS•S Standards: 2, 3, 4, 5)

PROFILE FOR TECHNOLOGY (ICT) LITERATE STUDENTS FOR GRADES 9–12

The following experiences with technology and digital resources are examples of learning activities in which students might engage during Grades 9–12 (ages 14–18):

Create and publish an online art gallery with examples and commentary that demonstrate an understanding of different historical periods, cultures, and countries. (related NETS•S Standards: 1, 2)

Model legal and ethical behaviors when using information and technology by properly selecting, acquiring, and citing resources. (related NETS•S Standards: 3, 5)

Create media-rich presentations for other students on the appropriate and ethical use of digital tools and resources. (related NETS•S Standards: 1, 5)

Further information regarding evaluation and assessment of digital story projects is provided in Chapter 5, including sample assessment rubrics. The complete set of student profiles can be found at www.iste.org/Content/NavigationMenu/NETS/ForStudents/2007Standards/Profiles/NETS_for_Students_2007_Profiles.htm.

Copyright and Citation

Because of its importance, an overview of copyright and citation is appropriate before we go any further. Copyright, as it applies to education, is the topic of many books and websites, some of which are presented here. Educators often don't understand that they do not have full freedom to just copy material and cite the copyright owner. Because of the potential ramifications of copyright law, many school districts are beginning to develop guidelines.

Guidelines and interpretations of the laws can vary widely from school to school (and even more so from country to country), so it is impractical, and outside the mission of this book, to strictly define what is acceptable and what is not. Nonetheless, it is important that from the beginning of the project, teachers insist that students know exactly where the text or multimedia elements for their digital story came from and how to locate the source. This is where copyright and citation join hands.

Copyright Rules in Education

Remember, knowledge of copyright rules in education is a must. For even the most experienced educator or administrator, copyright is a confusing and difficult subject to learn and to teach. Nonetheless, addressing copyright issues with students is a key element in meeting the digital citizenship standard in ISTE's NETS•S. Links to a wealth of copyright information are provided in the Resources section.

Photographs tend to be the most popular media element in student-generated digital stories. Following is common terminology regarding images and copyright. Images that are **public domain** are the least restricted for student use. Photographs taken during government projects are an example of acceptable public domain images, but students should be instructed to read the image usage guidelines. For example, the images in the "Image of the Day" archives of NASA (www. nasa.gov/multimedia/imagegallery/iotd_archive.html) are free for students to use, but the logo for NASA is not. There are also video and sound clips available for use on the NASA site.

Educational copyright rules have certain relaxations called **fair use**. Interpreting the provisions of the fair use doctrine isn't easy. Educators, administrators, and lawyers have opinions on what fair use allows ranging from nearly anything to almost nothing. At its most basic, fair use allows, in certain situations, educators and students to use a single image, a sound clip, or an extremely short music clip without paying for it, but only within the classroom walls. "Within the classroom walls" means that projects using those sources can't be shared with parents or other classrooms, shown in an auditorium, or burned to CD or DVD, and they can never be published on the web.

It is critical that you teach students that copyright is an automatic right. The creator does not need to apply for, label, or announce their copyright—it is applied automatically to any and all creative works at the moment of creation. Just because there is no copyright symbol or the owner is not identified, students can't assume that there aren't copyrights involved.

Much of the content found on the web is labeled with the owner's requirements for using the content. For example, Flickr, the photo-sharing website owned by Yahoo, allows users of this site to apply specific licenses to their work. Here are some examples of the general types of license agreements:

Royalty Free means that the images in question are available for a one-time purchase; then you may use them as you like.

Rights-Managed images are purchased only for a certain purpose for a specific period of time. The main point for royalty free and rights managed is that you must pay for them.

Noncommercial allows others to copy, distribute, display, and perform the work, as long as it is not for monetary gain. Derivative works (such as student-created digital stories) can be based on works covered by a noncommercial agreement.

No Derivative Works means the media elements can't be transformed in any way and must be used verbatim.

Share Alike allows distribution of derivative works based on the media elements, but only under a similar license.

Creative Commons

A new idea called Creative Commons has evolved to help people share under a newly defined set of licensing options. As a nonprofit organization, Creative Commons (http:// creativecommons.org) helps producers of media, text, and web pages "to grant some or all of their rights to the public while retaining others through a variety of licensing and contract schemes." Some of the media available through Creative Commons has been dedicated to the public domain or open content licensing terms. Now educators have a way to avoid potential problems with copyright laws that strictly guard the sharing of information.

Citation

Most schools have a preferred style of citation, and I recommend that teachers check the student handbook for mention of this. David Warlick's Citation Machine (http://citationmachine.net) is a good way to begin working with creating citations for middle school students. Library media specialists are also savvy about both citation and copyright, and classroom teachers should enlist their help and expertise for digital storytelling projects. Links to additional citation information are available in the Resources section.

Students who take their own photographs or make their own movies can gain a clear understanding of citation and the complications of copyright. Once they understand ownership, they are more likely to accept that they can't just take items from others without permission.

Resources

Writing Across the Curriculum

The Purdue Online Writing Lab: http://owl.english.purdue.edu

Web English Teacher: www.webenglishteacher.com

WritingFix: Writing Across the Curriculum:
www.writingfix.com/WAC.htm

The Writing Site: Writing Across the Curriculum:
www.thewritingsite.org/resources/curriculum

Writing Style and Techniques:
www.ipl.org/div/aplus/linkswritingstyle.htm

Digital Storytelling Related Podcasts

Tim Wilson, "The Savvy Technologist"
Blog: http://technosavvy.org

Wesley Fryer, "Moving at the Speed of Creativity"
Blog: www.speedofcreativity.org

Bernajean Porter

DigiTales: The Art of Telling Digital Stories (website):
www.digitales.us

DigiTales: The Art of Telling Digital Stories. (2005). Book available
through www.bjpconsulting.com/products/digitales

Joe Lambert

The Center for Digital Storytelling: www.storycenter.org

Digital Storytelling: Capturing Lives, Creating Communities,
2nd edition, The Center for Digital Storytelling. Book available
at http://store.storycenter.org

Expert Digital Storytelling Websites

DigiTales: The Art of Telling Stories: www.digitales.us

Center for Digital Story Telling: www.storycenter.org/index1.html

Marco Torres: Digital Storytelling:
http://homepage.mac.com/torres21

Australian Digital Story Websites

Australian Digital Storytelling:
http://innovateandintegrate.flexiblelearning.net.au

DigiTales Wiki: http://digitales.wikispaces.com

Digital Storytelling Network:
www.groups.edna.edu.au/course/view.php?id=107

Starter List of Ideas for Digital Storytelling

Digital Story Examples: www.storycenter.org/stories/

Tips for Digital Story Telling by Jon Orech:
www.techlearning.com/article/8030

Teach Digital: Curriculum by Wes Fryer:
http://teachdigital.pbwiki.com/digitalstorytelling

Telling Tales with Technology by Judy Salpeter:
www.techlearning.com/article/3536

Copyright

Copy Wrongs: www.edutopia.org/copyright/

Hall Davidson's Copyright Resources:
www.halldavidson.net/downloads.html

Copyright with CyberBee: www.cyberbee.com/copyrt.html

A Visit to Copyright Bay: www.stfrancis.edu/cid/copyrightbay

Managing Copyright in Schools: www.carolsimpson.com/
copyright/Managing_Copyright_for_Librarians.htm

Taking the Mystery out of Copyright:
www.loc.gov/teachers/copyrightmystery/#

Creative Commons FAQs: http://wiki.creativecommons.org/FAQ

Creative Commons Definitions:
http://creativecommons.org/about/licenses

Flickr: www.flickr.com/creativecommons

Citation

David Warlick's Citation Machine: http://citationmachine.net

University of Iowa Citation Styles:
www.uiowa.edu/~commstud/resources/citation.html

Nauset Public Schools Research and Style Manual: Works Cited for
Grades 1–6: http://nausetschools.org/research/works2.htm

Digital Story Preparation

I've divided the multistep process of combining text, voice, audio, images, and video to create and tell story into three stages: preparation, production, and presentation. I believe this represents the natural sequencing and division of the steps required, though the division is arbitrary. Although presentation is the final step, it is critical that it inform every aspect of planning and production. The process takes time, and teachers may want to apply assessments throughout the development.

During the preparation stage, teacher and students define their audience and determine what the final product will be (video or podcast) and how it will be presented (i.e., in class or posted to the web). They organize preliminary materials and plan for the digital storytelling project/assignment. The teacher will decide at this point whether to have students work as individuals, in small groups, or as a whole class. The teacher will also begin creation of a formative assessment (see Chapter 5). If the project is connected to standards-based curriculum, those elements are integrated into the assessment plan.

As part of preparation of the assignment, teachers may choose to create an introductory digital story about the topic and have students brainstorm ways to find meaning, point of view, or emotional connections of their own. Because classroom time is short and precious, teachers will want to define, at this stage, what class time will be dedicated to each stage, and also decide whether homework time is part of the preparation process. Similar decisions about time spent in class and time spent working independently by students will be made for each stage of the project.

The Emotional Connection

Classic storytellers craft their stories so that the telling of the story is part of the experience. The personal connection between audience and storyteller is emotionally charged with eye contact, body language, and narration. Depending on how adept the storyteller is at entrancing the audience, as well as how interested the audience is in the content of the story, the audience gets caught up in the experience. A great storyteller evokes an emotional connection. It is a magical and not easily forgotten experience.

There is magic in the experience for storytellers as well. Connecting with an audience and bringing them into the story can be a deeply satisfying experience—one that digital storytelling offers to students.

Educators who are interested in digital storytelling understand this connection and may have experienced this phenomenon themselves with a live-audience classic storyteller. It is this excited, participatory learning experience that every teacher wishes could be provided for every topic in the curriculum. But students do not always feel connected to and excited about learning. The digital storymaking process combined with solid curriculum benchmark lessons can help students make a connection to the material at hand.

In the visual aspects of digital storytelling, students can choose still images and video that make learning meaningful while meeting the needs of standards-based learning. Emotionally, music and sound effects can evoke personal memories and at the same time promote understanding of a time period or era. Combining auditory media with visual images can charge the story, offering the audience a magical experience like that created by the classic storyteller.

Digital storytelling requires students to consider their audience carefully. Keeping the audience clearly in mind—knowing their work will have an audience—can help engage students in a digital storytelling project.

The digital storytelling project has a dual focus, the story and the application of the technology. Although I assert the story is at the heart of the matter, I focus here primarily on the application of the technologies and related resources to support digital storytelling. During the preparation stage, the development and the processes of good writing should be highlighted in any case and addressed in the formative assessment rubric. These processes will inform the development of the storyboard.

Note: Guidelines for generating formative assessment rubrics can be found in Chapter 5 of this book.

Once the idea or concept of the story forms into something tangible, the planning process begins. Planning can be hard work, and students often find this part tedious. They will learn by trial and error that this step can't be bypassed. They will also discover that technology tools can help with the planning process. We'll take a look at some of these tools.

Timelines

Organizing and sequencing is a necessary part of the planning process. Having a visual timeline of people, dates, and places helps students organize their research, especially for projects that are historically or scientifically based. Even a simple timeline can help when the volume of material is too enormous for the length of a story. Digital stories are necessarily brief because of video storage limitations, and deciding what is important in the story is an important editing lesson.

Classic timelines are easily accomplished on paper. Timelines in this form can be difficult to share, but for many students, putting the beginnings of a digital storytelling project on paper can help prepare the them for using the software tools later on. The paper-based planning tool can be scanned and shared as a graphic.

I recommend two Web 2.0 tools for timeline creation: Xtimeline and Dipity. Because of the nature of Web 2.0 tools, both use shared collaborative space online and are designed for the creation and storage of user-created timelines. Although both are free, there is a registration process, and there may be a minimum age requirement as part of the terms of use of the site. Teachers who wish to use either tool need to check to see whether the school district's content filtering procedure will allow access to this tool. Students should be carefully supervised while using these sites, because there is advertising content on each page. After registering, browse the existing timelines to see if any are related to your assigned student projects. Because many timelines are not designed exclusively for education, teachers need to investigate these tools carefully before using them with students.

XTimeline

XTimeline's online tool (www.xtimeline.com) involves working with a tabbed interface. The Explore tab holds the timelines, grouped into six major categories. The Create tab allows users to design timelines. When completed, the timelines are stored for further editing under My Timelines. There is also a search box, useable for searching for existing timelines of topical interest. For example, a search for the keywords "Civil War" found 62 timelines. First on this list was "Seventh Period's US History Timeline." By examining this further, students can access ideas for placement of people and events in the right time sequence on a timeline.

> **Note:** This timeline process should not be confused with using the timeline feature of movie-making applications (see Chapter 3).

Dipity

Dipity (www.dipity.com) is an online tool that does a good job of placing events with dates on a timeline. This tool is especially effective when used in a whole-classroom project situation where the results are projected for all students to see. The teacher creates the timeline, giving the project a title such as "Seventh Period American History." An event window opens and each student, or group of students, adds their dates and topics. Events do not have to be entered in any order, as the Dipity interface will sequence them automatically.

If the class has been organized into small groups—for example, each studying an event with a curricular goal such as the "Causes Leading to the American Revolution"—Dipity will place the events into a cohesive, sequenced visual timeline. As you project this, the whole class can see what each group has been working on. With this big-picture visual overview, students can see how their individual piece of the story fits into the big picture as part of the historical timeline. For large-group presentations, teachers can have students present their digital stories in the order that the timeline suggests.

Dipity has the added feature of allowing an associated image with each event. Using this feature, students working in classroom groups might select a repeating image for their segment of the whole project timeline. The timelines created with Dipity can also be shared with classrooms globally, and vice versa, providing teachers and students with a chance to observe timelines on similar topics created by their cohorts.

> **Note:** Before using any timeline or storyboarding product, students should gather all of the facts and dates that may form part of their stories.

Concept Mapping

For organizing many types of projects, including digital stories, educators have found that students benefit from using concept mapping as a tool for "thinking it out." If students are working on a group digital storytelling project, where each person is assigned a particular part of the story to research and present to the group, this type of software can make the project workable for students of all abilities in the integrated classroom. The resource list at the end of this chapter provides links to websites for several examples of this software.

Inspiration Software

Most well-known are the software products made by Inspiration Software (www.inspiration.com), makers of Inspiration (Grade 6 to adult), InspireData (Grades 4–12), and Kidspiration (Grades K–5). These commercial software applications offer free trial periods and school licenses, and they may already be part of your school district's software library. The Inspiration website offers lessons, connections to standards, and technical support.

Gliffy

Gliffy (www.gliffy.com), a web-based diagramming software application, is named after the word *glyph*, a symbol or character that represents information in a nonverbal way. You must sign up to use this product. Although a free one-month trial is available, after that your school must pay for its use. The advantage of this product is the fact that it is online, giving your students access to it from any computer at school or at home.

Storyboards or Story Maps

Storyboards are used as a kind of graphic organizer. Whether on paper or on the computer screen, these are helpful tools for keeping students on track with any project. Many students may already be familiar with storyboarding. Examples of a storyboard visual include the classic comic strip and, in its expanded format, the popular graphic novel (see page 45).

Classically, storyboarding techniques included a set of index cards that could be arranged and rearranged as the story came to life. Multimedia-authoring software, such as HyperStudio and PowerPoint, has been used for both planning and presenting digital stories. The single-frame "slide" or "card" facilitates the same sort of index card planning in an electronic format. Story elements are generated either in a linear format or, for the

Ancestors who traveled to America to find a better life are part of the past of many of today's Americans. Finding out who they were, why they came here and what their lives were like is part of any study of family history.

This is the timeline of three brothers, John, James and Thomas, the "Brothers Broadfoot", who ventured to America from their native Scotland to begin new lives in America. Their father was a granite worker and all three brothers brought the skills of mining granite, making paving stones and carving monuments with them to America. This is their story...

Example of photo and text prepared for use in a storyboard

advanced user, in a nonlinear format. For several years now, this has been the standard of technology-based project planning. Even younger students, with teacher help, have created whole thematic class stories.

Storyboarding with PowerPoint

Students begin by authoring a single frame of a story by drawing a visual image with text on a single sheet of paper or on the computer screen. The teacher encourages students to follow the guidelines of the project. Students in elementary grades focus on their part of the assignment, as a piece of the whole, using the storyboarding method. Teachers can use a blank presentation printout for younger students to use at their desk along with a project guidelines rubric. The rubric guides the student in simple planning prior to work on the computer.

Follow these steps to use PowerPoint for storyboarding:

1. Launch PowerPoint and create at least two blank or empty slides.

2. Use the Print dialog box (Ctrl-P, or choose Print from the File menu), not the toolbar print icon, to locate the Handout feature of PowerPoint.

3. In the Print dialog box, look for the "Print what" drop-down section and choose Handouts. In the Handouts section, look for the "Slides per page" drop-down section, then choose 2 to create two blank slides per printout. (You can choose another number, depending on how many boxes you would like in your printout.)

4. Click to place a checkmark next to "Frame slides" to create a boundary line around the empty boxes. Click Print to send this to your printer.

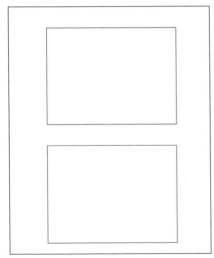

PowerPoint's Print dialog box

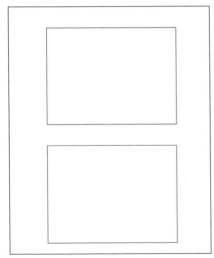

A blank printable PowerPoint storyboard

Annette Lamb's Sequential Art, Graphic Novels and Comics Class

Designed for her graduate classes, Annette Lamb's web pages— Sequential Art, Graphic Novels and Comics (http://eduscapes. com/sessions/comics/)—define sequential art as "a category of illustration that includes cartoons, comics, graphic novels, and manga." Cartoons and comics are familiar to most adults and are widely read today in newspapers, websites, and in books. Graphic novels are a step away from the comic book as they are quite lengthy and well-scripted, and the pictures are either computer generated or hand drawn and scanned for publication.

Many young teens are captivated by graphic novels. To them, the text is just as important as the illustration, and many aspire to be graphic novelists. Manga is a comic drawn in a Japanese style and may be the first reading material that students encounter that reads top to bottom and right to left. Young adult reading groups in public libraries are filled with teens of both sexes who find manga wildly fascinating. This is why Lamb, a library-media specialist, devotes several web pages of information, lessons, and tools to help librarians and educational technology specialists work with this genre of digital storytelling.

Comic Life (Macintosh, Windows) and Comic Touch (for iPhone/iPod touch) are downloadble commercial applications that you can use to work with this type of story art. These products are availalbe at http://plasq.com/products/. A 30-day trial of Comic Life is available.

For those teachers seeking storyboard templates or examples of planning sheets, the web has some gems, and you will find some of those in the Resources section. In addition to a simple web search for the definition of storyboard or story map, try a phrase search for "storyboard planning sheets." Some will be in the easily printed Adobe portable document format (PDF), some are PowerPoint templates for print or use from within PowerPoint, and some are web pages.

Searching for storyboard resources with Google's advanced search

StoryBoard Pro Software

Storyboarding has been made accessible for everyone with the free downloadable software resource StoryBoard Pro (http://movies.atomiclearning.com/k12/storyboardpro/), published by Atomic Learning. The software, available for both Macintosh and Windows users, comes with a series of free online tutorials (http://movies.atomiclearning.com/k12/storytellingindex.shtml).

Designed for those who wish to make movies for digital storytelling, these brief tutorials are a big help.

Atomic Learning offers this product for free in hopes that you will enjoy this type of online tutorial experience and purchase one or more of their other numerous software product tutorials. There's also a free preview of a "Video Storytelling Guide," recommended for digital storytellers using video for their storytelling presentation experience.

Script Writing

Students may be dismayed to discover that digital story development requires writing a story and following the time-honored tenets of good writing. Script writing is hard work for most students. Collaborative scripts may require even more work. Writing a script for a story is not blog writing, text messaging, or typing text onto the slides of multimedia software; it is work. Students need to be aware of this difference.

Word Processing Tools

Naturally, the word processor is the tool of choice. Although Microsoft's Word is by far the most commonly known and used word processor on both Macintosh and Windows platforms, there are many other options. Open-source products such as Open Office include many of the same features found in Microsoft's suite and are compatible in many ways. Even built-in word processing applications, such as WordPad (part of Windows), are quite acceptable alternatives for this level of work.

Google Docs

There are many new online word processing tools. Google Docs, for example, is a free suite of word processing, spreadsheet, and presentation applications designed for collaboration. Because the resulting work is stored online, students can access their work from any location—school, library, or home. A Google account is required, but it is a no-cost alternative to students using different word processing software applications and having to e-mail their scripts to each other. Because Google Docs also has a presentation tool, students can use that as a stored collaborative space simulating a storyboard tool.

Google Docs also provides the Google Gears plug-in, a way for users to work on their documents stored by Google Docs even when they are offline. This is great news for those teachers who have students working on digital stories where access to the Internet is not always available.

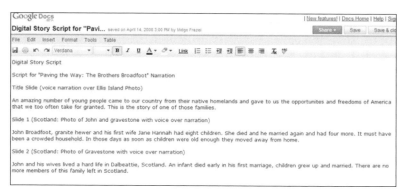

Google Docs script screenshot

Google Tools for Digital Storytelling

Google Docs

http://docs.google.com

Account Sign-up: www.google.com/accounts/NewAccount

Google for Educators: www.google.com/educators

Help Page: http://docs.google.com/support

Google Docs is a free suite of online word processing, spreadsheet, and presentation applications that can be used to create individual or collaborative documents, spreadsheets, and presentations with as many features as most desktop applications. These created products can be downloaded to your computer to be used offline, or stored and shared with others online. To use them, all you have to do is sign up for a free Google account, and you can access the suite, the instructions, a video tutorial, and a special online section with shared ideas for educators.

Google Gears

http://gears.google.com

Help Page: http://tinyurl.com/5mjm4u

If you want to work with the products you create with Google Docs when you're not online, you will be prompted to install a small plug-in, called Google Gears. It is easy and free. Just follow the directions contained on the Google Docs Help page.

Google Notebook

http://google.com/notebook

Notebook Tour: www.google.com/googlenotebook/tour1.html

Google Notebook is an online tool designed to gather and store information from web pages. These items can be snippets of text, images, links (URLs), and text that you will want to type in and save. It is meant to simulate a physical notebook with a pocket for storing items. Teachers and students can use this handy tool privately or as a shared resource for group projects such as digital storytelling.

Google Image Search

http://images.google.com

Google Image Search service is a way to locate images stored on web pages quickly by performing a keyword search. It should be noted that copyright rules apply to using these photographs and images no matter where they are located. Students should be instructed to look for the owner of the image and to find a way to contact them if permission is needed.

Google Maps

http://maps.google.com

Google Maps mapping service is an online tool for displaying maps of locations near and far. Place-based digital stories rely on the use of maps so that students can relate the visual map with the locations in the story. Ever improving, Google Maps is a wonderful and useful classroom tool. All stories, real or imagined, have locations to be explored, and this can help students develop essential geography skills.

Shared Media Resources

Many resources for multimedia are available under Creative Commons licenses, discussed in Chapter 1. Some are in the public domain or are offered under an open content license, meaning that they are freely available for use in student projects.

Educators, too, are taking photographs, making music and sounds, and applying the least restrictive Creative Commons license to their work so that others can use it legally. This way, if one teacher takes a photograph of an outdoor public monument, the photo can be shared with other educators whose students are writing digital stories about that monument and never had the opportunity to visit it in person. The most commonly used repository is hosted by Tech4Learning and is called Pics4Learning (www.pics4learning.com). Photographs are grouped by subject. If you don't find what you're looking for, you can search the collection. Information is also provided at Pics4Learning to assist students with citation.

In contrast, morgueFile's repository of high-resolution photographs (http://morguefile.com) can be searched by keyword, but each search result should be examined carefully for appropriate school use and for copyright information. This is also true for images in Google's Image Search (http://images. google.com). If a student finds a photograph they'd like to use for their project, they must seek permission (by e-mail) from the person who owns it.

Recently, The Library of Congress and Flickr have teamed up to host photographs that have "no known copyright restrictions." This growing endeavor, called The Commons, (www.flickr.com/commons/) is an example of collaboration to make it easier to view historical photographs. Other museums and repositories of photographs with no restrictions on them may follow. This is great news for digital storytellers whose projects revolve around history and culture.

The Commons—Historical Photo Archive

An exciting development for teachers, students, historians, archivists, librarians, and other digital denizens is the recent partnership formed between the Library of Congress and Flickr. The result is a giant collection of historical photos with "no known copyright restrictions." The partnership was launched as a pilot project in January of 2008 with a collection of about 1,500 photos selected from over a million photos from the Library of Congress. This archive is known as The Commons (www.flickr.com/commons/).

Sample Commons photograph

Users can tag photos freely, and they can also contribute photos. Although the collection is still growing, this brilliant idea has caught on like wildfire. People spend hours examining, commenting on, and tagging photos for use in all kinds of projects. If you visit their site you'll see that today there are as many as 20 million tags on this Flickr site.

Also, take a look at the cultural artifacts (moving images, live music archives, and audio) at the Internet Archive (www.archive. org) to find project-appropriate resources. This site also offers a search forum bulletin board on the front page, with date and time of the post.

The Open Video Project (www.open-video.org) holds only video clips, but is likewise education-friendly. This site is sponsored by the University of North Carolina. The listings, organized by genre, provide length, color, and sound details.

Podcasting and Audio Files

Podcasting is a way to share and receive audio broadcasts through the Internet. Using digital media files, podcasts can be an effective way to tell digital stories. Sound clips and short musical clips are being created and posted via podcasts on websites with the expressed intent of sharing the material with students. Use caution with any of these sites because the word "free" is beginning to mean different things to different people. Check also for rights to educational use.

Freeplay Music has an excellent libary of clips of music in different lengths, perfect for digital storytelling, but these clips may not be broadcast. You may not post them to the web as part of your project or in podcasts—as many educators once thought—even in abbreviated format, but they are great for in-classroom projects.

Educators may also be interested in two music and sound clip sites that contain content licensed under Creative Commons. ccMixter (http://ccmixter.org) is a community music site featuring music remixes licensed under Creative Commons. The Freesound Project (www.freesound.org) is a collaborative database of Creative Commons licensed sounds (not music) for use in audio tracks and podcasts.

Additional sites are listed in the Resources section at the end of this chapter.

Illustration Tool

Tech4 Learning, a popular educational software company, created Twist (www.tech4learning.com/twist/), an affordable vector-based illustration tool to be used in Grades 3–12 to create scientific diagrams and other drawings for digital stories that have their curriculum connection to science and technology. Students can design images that can be easily exported to common graphic formats, then easily inserted into other applications to create the story's technology connection.

A quick look at the company's website will demonstrate the flexibility of this application. Twist sample files can be downloaded and opened in this application as a start for digital storytelling projects. Younger students in Grades 3–5 can create a single image to be placed in the digital story as part of a project or to be used as a story starter to open the conversation between teacher and student within a curriculum area. In addition, educators around the world have freely donated images and photographs that can be used as starters for the background of Twist illustrations.

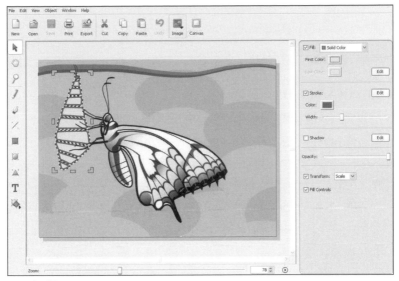

Example of Twist project screen

Resources

Timelines

Chronological Timeline: www.teachervision.fen.com/
graphic-organizers/printable/6301.html

Dipity: www.dipity.com

ReadWriteThink Interactive Timeline:
www.readwritethink.org/materials/timeline

Timeline Generator:
www.teach-nology.com/web_tools/materials/timelines

Timeline Graphic Organizer:
www.eduplace.com/graphicorganizer/pdf/timeline.pdf

XTimeline: www.xtimeline.com

Concept Mapping

Gliffy: www.gliffy.com

Inspiration software: www.inspiration.com

Storyboards

Comic Life and Comic Touch software: http://plasq.com/products

Print Free Storyboards: www.pdfpad.com/storyboards

Storyboard Example:
www.sdcoe.k12.ca.us/SCORE/actbank/tboard.htm

Storyboard Planning PowerPoint Template:
www.alice.org/bvw03/TAweb/storyboard_template.ppt

StoryBoard Pro Software:
http://movies.atomiclearning.com/k12/storyboardpro

StoryBoard Pro free tutorials:
http://movies.atomiclearning.com/k12/storytellingindex.shtml

Storyboarding: A Recipe:
www.storycenter.org/memvoice/pages/tutorial_3.html

Shared Resources for Image and Video

Pics4Learning: www.pics4learning.com

morgueFile: http://morguefile.com

Google Image Search: http://images.google.com

The Commons: www.flickr.com/commons

Internet Archive: www.archive.org

The Open Video Project: www.open-video.org

Audio Clips

PodSafe Audio: www.podsafeaudio.com

Partners in Rhyme: Free Sound Effects:
www.partnersinrhyme.com/pir/PIRsfx.shtml.
Note that many sound effects are royalty free rather than free—a license fee must still be paid.

Freeplay Music: www.freeplaymusic.com

Musopen: www.musopen.com
Free public domain classical music.

ccMixter: http://ccmixter.org
A community music site featuring music remixes licensed under Creative Commons.

The Freesound Project: http://www.freesound.org
A collaborative database of Creative Commons licensed sounds.

Digital Story Production

During the production stage, all the media elements of the story are brought together and are rendered into a video format (movie) or an audio format (podcast). At the beginning of this stage, the teacher presents the plan for students to locate, evaluate, select, and properly cite the multimedia elements that will be used. This is the longest of the project stages. For the students, it is often the most enjoyable. For group projects, different students can assume the roles of writer, director, producer, or actor, much as in filmmaking. The teacher should actively mentor both individual and group work. This is also the point where an informal evaluation may be employed.

I recommend testing the technology you will be using to make sure it's in working order before the students begin. Students may need to learn troubleshooting when plans don't go as expected, and these activities can be assessed as part of the group's rubric under the heading of digital citizenship.

Teaming with a technology specialist in your school and having students devote time in the computer lab should be arranged whenever possible.

Note: If students use iMovie or Movie Maker for their digital story, this can add time to the project because video file editing can be a relatively slow process. Teachers should take this into account during their planning.

Students' enthusiasm for digital storytelling may sometimes lead them to go overboard with the use of too much animation, too many photographs, and too much camera motion—such as pan and zoom. This is especially common with students who are already familiar with the process of making movies, and the result can be sensory overload for the audience. Students who have had a lot of experience on their own also tend to spend an extraordinary amount of time on the special effects. I suggest helping these video enthusiasts focus on writing or narrating the story. These students are often a valuable asset to the teacher and can be asked to peer teach other less experienced students.

The production stage of digital story creation can be enhanced with the use of low-cost or no-cost software products. Although many excellent high-end applications are available, most curriculum and production goals can be met with free or inexpensive media tools, and you'll find these listed throughout this book.

It would be impossible to create a resource list of all available media resources, hardware, and software applications you could use with digital storytelling. However, even with the limited number of resources I've chosen to include in this book, you will be able to get started. What is offered here is meant to expose you to the possibilities. Most of these media resources are useable with the newer multimedia-based desktop or laptop computers used in education; most work with both Macintosh and Windows operating systems. Many schools have a few digital cameras available for student use that most likely can create digital video clips as well as still photographs.

Locating and Evaluating Media to Use in the Digital Story

Locating and evaluating the media elements for the digital stories often turns out to be an exciting adventure in learning online. Many teachers prefer to have their students take their own photographs, use hand-drawn and scanned illustrations of their own design, or use a graphic software package to create the digital images. Many students are adept at composing their own music. Teaching students about their rights as producers of media is a great way to show them how to be ethical and responsible consumers of media.

Posting graphics to a photo-sharing website is a good lesson in archiving and organizing materials for proper citation and credit. If you are managing many individuals or groups of students working on digital storytelling projects, the mentoring process should include the teaching of research skills, plus the tasks of organizing and citing gathered resources.

Creating their own media consumes more valuable classroom minutes, but it is often more engaging for students than using stock media. Additionally, it often results in just the right piece and avoids any copyright issues.

If media is captured on the Internet, or in hardcopy, students are required to use proper citation methods and be aware of any copyright issues for the media involved. Insist that students know exactly where they found the media elements. Making this clear should be part of the formative assessment process. Students can keep track of media elements, web pages, and text found online by creating a Google Notebook. (See Google Tools for Digital Storytelling, on page 49.)

iMovie

iMovie from Apple was the among the first affordable desktop video production applications, making digital home movie editing accessible for the average person. It is part of the iLife suite of applications on Macintosh systems. Like many applications for the Mac, iMovie doesn't have a steep learning curve to overcome. User information on the iMovie website is well organized and even enticing. They offer a series of movies demonstrating how easy it is to make a movie.

This software will help you and your students organize movie clips, and add titles, transitions, and voiceovers. The application is user-friendly and has earned my seal of approval. More information on iMovie can be found at www.apple.com/ilife/imovie/.

Creating an iMovie with Kathy Schrock

Kathy Schrock, world-renowned and respected educational technologist, created a digital story, "Winter on Cape Cod," to demonstrate and share how easy digital storytelling can be with iMovie. She shares with us here some screen shots from her production process and her storyboard. She demonstrates how she assembled the photos and video clips and then opened iMovie, imported the photos, and completed the process.

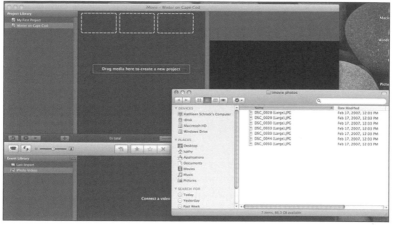

Importing photos into iMovie

After arranging the clips and the photos from her storyboard, she imported a photo to use for the opening title. A title slide is important, because it must capture the attention of the audience, should be pleasing to look at, and should also be displayed a bit longer than other slides. The title slide holds the title text and the author's name, and it should be on-screen when any narration begins. Occasionally, this first title slide can also be the visual for opening music. After this slide, the audience views the media elements and experiences the auditory part of the story.

Opening title slide

Note that the length of time the media elements are displayed should be adjusted to suit the length of the auditory and text portions. Some stories are improved with the addition of special effects such as screen transitions to enhance the mood and to give the audience time to absorb the story.

After tweaking, viewing, and saving the story, the resulting product should be rendered to a movie format, or more specifically into a video file format viewable in software that

Setting times and transitions in iMovie

plays video. Most computers are already equipped with software that plays video formats, such as QuickTime, RealPlayer, or Windows Movie Maker.

Once the movie is burned onto a CD or DVD, or uploaded to a website, it can be played and shared with an audience. You can find out more about this process at iMovie's "Share" menu.

iMovie Export Menu

Learning in Hand

On his Learning in Hand website (http://learninginhand.com), education consultant Tony Vincent offers a workshop for educators and posts his resources for moviemaking. You will find Tony's handouts, storyboard page, and online presentation useful for other video-based projects in addition to his ideas for storytelling.

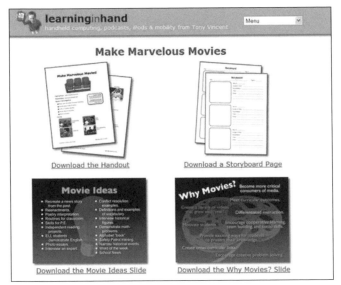

Tony Vincent's movie-making resources web page

Terrific for computer users on all platforms, Tony's handouts are a valuable resource. He offers experience in the classroom and has taught his own students good video and still camera techniques, no matter what level of camera experience they may have had.

Photo Story and Movie Maker

Not to be outdone by Apple's successful desktop video-editing application, Microsoft offers Photo Story and Movie Maker, two free tools for digital storytelling that are already installed on computers running Windows XP or Windows Vista. If you find they are not installed, both are freely available from Microsoft's website for quick download. Photo Story can be found at www.microsoft.com/windowsxp/using/digitalphotography/ photostory/ and Movie Maker at www.microsoft.com/ windowsxp/downloads/updates/moviemaker2.mspx.

The primary difference between Photo Story and Movie Maker is that Photo Story does not allow importation of video clips. But, you can make a digital story in Photo Story, render it to movie format, and import it into Movie Maker. You can add digital story elements either before or after this imported movie. Of course, you can use either product to complete your digital story.

Photo Story

Photo Story shines as a digital storytelling application, in part because it creates video from still digital images. It is also a favorite choice of educators for ePortfolio creation because, for example, they can use scanned or digital photographs taken of paper projects and then import the photos into Photo Story.

Another advantage of Photo Story is that you can attach a microphone to your desktop computer or laptop and easily record and store short narration. Photo Story also offers copyright-free music in many styles, which is easily applied to your project for a nice effect. For busy teachers who don't have the classroom time to record and edit small narrations, or to hunt for just the right noncopyrighted music, Photo Story is a great resource.

Following is a tutorial that will introduce you to the capabilities of Photo Story.

Photo Story Tutorial

Imagine that your students are working with the local Chamber of Commerce to produce a print and online project with a focus on family-owned businesses. As part of this, your students must produce a digital story about the history of each business, demonstrating to a community audience how each business has evolved over time. Your students have scanned old photographs and brochures, enhanced the resulting images, and conducted and recorded oral interviews from people in the community who worked for and lived near the business. They have developed a timeline and created a simple storyboard as a first step in the production process. After completion of this part of the project, students will take photographs of the business as it exist today, and then use Photo Story to blend together the history, the oral interviews, and the pictures of the current business into a single production. The resulting digital story will show changes in perspectives over time. This project, by the way, meets national and state standards in history. At the same time, it helps students connect to their own community.

In the tutorial that follows, screenshots and instructions are for Photo Story 3. Both older and yet-to-be-released versions will differ somewhat, but should maintain the same basic functionality.

Importing photos for the project

1.   Students place scanned and edited photos and documents into a folder titled with the name of the project.

2.   Students open Photo Story, and at the first on-screen choice select Begin a New Story.

3.   Students then click the Next button.

4.   The next screen, called the "Import and arrange your pictures" screen, asks students to Import Pictures.

5.   When students click on the Import Pictures button, the file browser opens, allowing them to import one, some, or all of the photos into the folder.

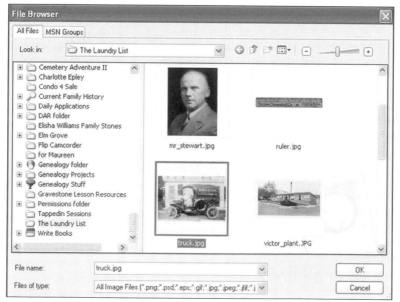

Importing photos into Photo Story

Arranging and editing photos

6. Next, students bring the still images into a timeline, where they can be easily rearranged by dragging or be deleted. Photo Story provides tools for simple editing techniques. Go to the Edit menu or find other tools located directly underneath each image.

7. Students may need assistance in order to understand the process of removing black borders.

8. At this point, it is critical that students name and save the project. This is not the same as rendering a movie, as that comes later in the process.

   The buttons at the bottom of each screen allow projects to be saved frequently, and also permit students to return to a previous screen if needed.

Arranging photos in Photo Story

Adding titles and effects to photos

9. The "Add a title to your pictures" screen provides text overlay on any image and, as shown in the following figure, allows students to add a small amount of text to any slide, especially to a first or title slide. An important note for teachers: there is no spelling checker in this application, so all text should be checked manually.

10. Familiarize your students with the Customize Motion options Motion and Duration, and Transition.

11. Have students learn how to lengthen the time each slide is displayed on screen (at least 7 seconds is needed). They can also control the Ken Burns Effect of panning and zooming.

12. Students can click the Transition tab to apply or remove transitions and to select a transition type.

13. Teachers, be sure to work with all of these tools beforehand to decide how students can best take advantage of all the special effects.

Adding text to a slide in Photo Story

Adding transitions in Photo Story

Adding narration and other sound

14. At this point in the program, students will have the option of adding narration. (They will need a microphone to record the narration.)

15. Background music can be applied and previewed at the next screen. The Create Music button is for applying the wide variety of prepackaged music. The volume of the music can be adjusted here.

Digital stories that incorporate special effects, music, and narration will naturally take students longer to produce.

Adding music in Photo Story

Creating the project video

16. At this point, students should stop and save their story as a project (a WP3 file), prior to creating the video. If they skip this step, they can't return to make changes, corrections, or adjustments. So, insist on this saving step before students move to the final screen! Students will probably need mentoring during this process.

17. Rendering the digital story into a movie format is the final step. Before they do, students should read about the choices available by clicking on the link "Learn more about the selected choices," which quickly opens the Help file to the correct page. Please note that as students click on each choice of how to save the movie file, an explanation of its technical requirements appears.

18. Most of the time, students save their movie using the "Save your story for playback on the computer" option. When specifying the location and filename of the story, saving movies to the My Videos folder within the My Documents folder is the logical choice and helps students locate the project at a later time.

19. When students are ready to render the project into a movie file format, they should click the Next button. This process can take some time depending on the file's size, so plan accordingly. It is not something that can be accomplished in the few seconds before the end of a class period.

Saving story to movie format in Photo Story

Movie Maker

Movie Maker from Microsoft is a more complex application than Photo Story, but after you have created your first digital story— including the ePortfolio or photo essay variations—in Photo Story you will be ready to work with Movie Maker. Remember that movies rendered with Photo Story can be inserted into Movie Maker as part of a larger production.

Like iMovie on the Macintosh, Movie Maker is a full-featured video-editing and production application. This means that students will have many more options for manipulating and controlling the content. Although this can further empower many students, the extra complexity can get in the way of others. Additionally, video is much more demanding of computer resources than still images. You'll want to set aside more time for students to experiment with the application, but you'll also need to ensure you have ample storage space for the video and working files.

Movie Maker Tutorial

Imagine that your students are involved in learning about the pilgrims who traveled to America seeking religious freedom in a new world. One of the goals of your month-long classroom unit is for students to understand what hardships, fears, and emotions these travelers faced in their journey of survival.

As part of this, your students must create a virtual fieldtrip to modern day Plymouth, Massachusetts, connecting the past with the present for a better understanding of history.

For the preparation stage, students consider how the telling and retelling of these stories has created legends, mistruths, and modern-day controversies.

Students investigate the "That's Plymouth Rock?" WebQuest for background material (www.midgefrazel.net/wqprock.html) then develop a timeline and create a story board as part of the production process.

In the steps that follow, screenshots and instructions for Movie Maker are for version 2. The older and yet-to-be-released versions will differ, but should maintain the same basic functionality.

Importing photos for the project

1. Students gather needed media elements to create their digital story and place them into a folder titled with the name of the project.

2. Students open Movie Maker 2. From the File menu, they choose Import into Collections.

3. Students use the Import File dialog box that appears to navigate to the location of the student folder.

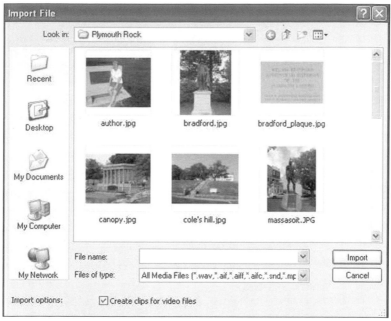

Importing photos into Movie Maker

4. Students choose the files they are going to use, and then click Import.

5. Once their files appear in their project, students save and name their project by pulling down the File menu and choosing "Save Project as…."

6. The Collection panel in the center of the screen holds the media elements for the movie project. These elements can be added to the timeline at the bottom of the screen by using drag and drop. Students can add more media elements to this panel by using the same method of importing them into their collection.

7. At this point, saving the project again is essential.

Example Timeline view in Movie Maker

Arranging and editing photos

8. The timeline at the lower part of the screen is the heart of the process of creating the movie. Students drag and drop the elements (photos, sound clips, and music) from their Collection panel into the timeline area. Media items can be rearranged by dragging.

9. Each visual element can be viewed by clicking on it to have it appear in the Monitor pane. Students can also view the movie using the Play button in this Monitor pane.

10. The bar in the timeline will move, showing where students currently are in the viewing of the movie.

Adding titles and effects to photos

11. Text slides can be placed at any point in a story. Each movie should include at least a title slide and a slide for credits at the end.

12. Students can type special text slides, like the poem shown, in PowerPoint and export them as a JPEG file to be used in the story.

13. Text slide display time must be lengthened to give the audience ample opportunity to read the text or the purpose will be lost.

14. Students should explore the choices available through the Tools menu.

Title and Credits—Movie Maker

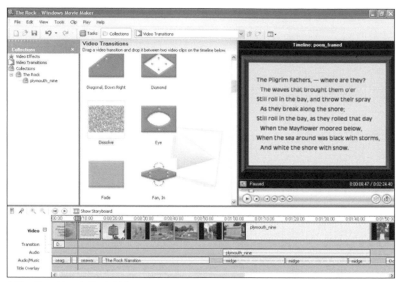

Adding Transitions in Movie Maker

15. Students can apply special effects, such as transitions, to enhance the mood of their story, but these should be used sparingly. Transitions will appear in the transitions line of the timeline so they can easily be moved or deleted as needed.

16. Movie clips can be added, and if the sound that accompanies the video is not essential to the story, that track can be muted (by right-clicking the audio track in the timeline and choosing Mute from the contextual menu). By doing this, students can use a voice-over narration, or music, with the motion of the video, easing concerns about background chatter.

Creating the project video

17. Saving the project before rendering the story to video format is important, because no changes can be made to the movie once it is created. But, if the project is saved correctly, the project files can be opened in Movie Maker again, changes made, and another movie rendered.

18. When students are ready to create the movie file, they should pull down the File menu and choose "Save Movie File...." The "Learn more about saving movie files" link will help explain what the choices are.

19. Students should give the movie a name, choose a saving location, and wait while the story is rendered into a movie.

20. The movie will be playable in Windows Media Player.

Rendering to a movie format in Movie Maker

More Creativity Tools for Production

Although most digital stories can be produced and presented with applications and tools readily available and affordable for the classroom, it is wise for teachers to examine new creative tools. There are plenty of choices in commercial software for photo editing and video editing with pricing well under $100. Although iMovie and Movie Maker are more than capable free products, offerings from Adobe, Sony, Pinnacle, Corel, and others can add valuable and fun features and capabilities, especially for somewhat older and more advanced students.

In addition to commercial software, there are a number of web-based products that can fit into your digital storytelling bag of tricks. A couple I really like are Bubbleshare and Picnik.

Bubbleshare

Bubbleshare (www.bubbleshare.com) is an online tool for sharing photo-based slide shows. It's a cool program and can promote student interest in photography. Bubbleshare helps groups of students decide which photographs are important to their stories. It's not unusual for this selection process to take students a long time as they decide which photos will have the most impact with their story. The more simple the story, the less time it will take.

Picnik

Picnik (www.picnik.com) is an online photo-editing tool. It is easy to use, and it works well with photos hosted online and with photos stored on the computer. There is a free version that provides basic photo manipulation, helping students move quickly through the process of resizing, enhancing, and saving photographs for their stories.

Creating and Editing Audio Files

Audio files are essential components of digital storytelling, whether they accompany a series of images or, as in podcasts, make up the digital story itself. Some useful podcasting websites are listed in the Resources section at the end of this chapter.

The value of sound is not to be underestimated even in visually based digital storytelling. Students should relate the music to the story, rather than just adding their favorite music clips. Remember, the point is to convey story with the use of just the right combination of digital components. Sound effects can also be a nice addition, as long as they don't detract from the narration or the music. Students tend to go overboard, enthusiastically adding sound effects, music, and narration to every project.

In addition to standing alone as digital stories, podcasts can serve as a supplement or extension to a visually told digital story, and as a source for gathering narrations. Podcasts can be created using inexpensive microphones to capture narration or interviews in MP3 format. This digital file can then be enhanced with sound effect clips or music.

Audacity

Audacity (http://audacity.sourceforge.net) is a free, open source sound editor application that is commonly used for recording narration and editing music. It is a cross-platform application and is virtually identical in use for Macintosh, Windows, and Linux users. Users download the application for their computer platform from the information under the application's Download tab. Users will want to visit the Audacity Wiki page listed under the Help tab. Here you will find tutorials and excellent directions for creating a simple podcast using Audacity. Audacity-related tutorials, tips, and instructions can be found at https://academictech.doit.wisc.edu/orfi/avs/Modules/audacity.htm.

Be sure to download the LAME MP3 encoder (http://lame.sourceforge.net) so that you can export your music or podcast as an MP3 file. This encoder is a plug-in, so install it to the Audacity folder inside the Plug-ins folder.

Audacity's audio-editing environment

Resources

Production

iMovie: www.apple.com/ilife/imovie

Learning in Hand (Tony Vincent): http://learninginhand.com

Photo Story: www.microsoft.com/windowsxp/using/ digitalphotography/photostory/

Movie Maker: www.microsoft.com/windowsxp/downloads/ updates/moviemaker2.mspx

"That's Plymouth Rock?" WebQuest: www.midgefrazel.net/wqprock.html

Creativity Tools for Production

Bubbleshare: www.bubbleshare.com

Picnik: www.picnik.com

Audacity: http://audacity.sourceforge.net

Audacity-related tutorials, tips, and instructions: https:// academictech.doit.wisc.edu/orfi/avs/Modules/audacity.htm

LAME MP3 encoder: http://lame.sourceforge.net

Podcasting

Poducate Me: Podcasting in Education: www.poducateme.com

Podcasting: How to Create a Podcast: www.voices.com/podcasting.html

Podcasting Tools: www.podcasting-tools.com

Lessons Learned about Podcasting Microphones: www.speedofcreativity.org/2008/01/06/lessons-learned-about- podcasting-microphones

Digital Story
Presentation

In the past, classroom presentations took the form of students in front of the room reciting memorized facts, poems, songs, and speeches. People who had natural charisma and self-confidence found presenting their ideas, questions, and stories an easy task. But that's not so for all of us! Many of us quivered in fear when we were called upon to stand up in front of our classmates and perform this ancient and agonizing ritual. The sad truth is that this methodology did not foster understanding of the material. What's more, it was often graded by the student's ability to memorize a speech and to deliver it in a loud, clear voice.

Digital storytelling enables you to set up the presentation experience for students in a variety of ways that can be differentiated to challenge students' varied abilities. A digital story presented on a computer in the classroom must still be introduced by the student or students who produced it. A story burned onto a DVD for viewing outside the classroom, or one posted online, requires a different set of presentation skills. Recorded narration still requires some of the same speaking skills as a face-to-face presentation.

Face-to-face presentation skills continue to be valuable to students as preparation for their future careers. But the ability to present oneself to a remote audience, whether they are viewing the presentation on a DVD or over the web, is a real-world skill that is gaining in importance every year.

> **Note:** It's been demonstrated over and over that the process of sharing their work with others gives students extra motivation to write, develop, and publish their words in new and creative ways.

Students not only must know what type of presentation is expected of them, but also must consider their audience, right from the beginning of the digital storytelling process. If this important step in the preparation stage gets overlooked in the excitement of producing the story, presentations will greatly suffer.

Face-to-Face Audience

It may be necessary for students' digital stories to be presented only to a face-to-face audience. Many school policies state that student work is to be used only within the confines of the classroom or school. Presenting to peers helps prepare students for the times in their lives when they will be required to showcase their work and their abilities. Adhering to policy is also an important life lesson for students.

Introducing the digital story to the audience and responding to feedback are important parts of digital story presentation. Students should be prepared to introduce and describe their digital stories, and to answer questions about them after the audience sees the production. This requires strong oral presentation skills.

The following are some important presentation strategies that all students should learn and practice:

- Dress appropriately—appearance counts (neat and clean matters more than style)

- Plan and write a short introduction (script on note cards or cue cards)

- Make eye contact

- Speak with a strong voice

- Practice with a friend first

- Smile!

For an audience that will be face-to-face, in the classroom, the formative rubric should reflect the students' understanding of the importance of audience. Rubrics are discussed in detail in Chapter 5.

As part of the assessment process, students need clear guidelines on presentation expectations. Students should demonstrate their understanding of the importance of the project by considering their appearance, their posture, and their voice as part of this process. Taking pride in their work and having a sense of the audience reaction is part of the learning process, even if it is not directly assessed. Excellent advice for honing presentation skills can be found at the website for Princeton University's McGraw Center (http://web.princeton.edu/sites/mcgraw/oral_presentation_skills.html).

In addition to oral presentation skills, students should also learn and adhere to sound computer presentation skills. The following tips can be used as a checklist for computer presentations.

Tips for Computer Presentations

- Power strip is connected to the wall outlet and is powered on

- Presentation computer is plugged in and starts up

- Digital story (in movie format) is on the hard drive

- Digital story (in movie format) opens with software on hard drive

- For stories posted on the web: Internet connection is up and works with computer

- Digital story that has been posted to web opens and plays, then exits properly

- Classroom projection device is plugged in

- Classroom projection device is connected to computer

- External powered speakers are connected if needed for sound/music/narration

- Projected image can be clearly seen by audience

Remote Audience

Digital stories lend themselves to remote presentation, where the student is not there to introduce or explain the work. In some cases, digital stories can be burned onto CD or DVD and taken home by the student, or perhaps they will be shown to the entire school during an assembly. In other cases, where appropriate, digital stories can be posted and shared online. As mentioned earlier, public presentation of student work is always contingent upon school policy.

In any of these cases, there is a different skill set for presentation of the digital story. In these remote settings, obviously it isn't possible for a teacher to assess the student's presentation in the same manner as in a face-to-face environment. Instead, assessment can focus on the presentation within the digital story itself. Are student narrations delivered in a tone and with a vocabulary that aligns with and is appropriate to the audience?

If the audience is to be online, the teacher should monitor the feedback through the comments section of the online medium.

Note: Even if it is to be posted online, the digital story can also be archived—and I recommend this—onto a CD or DVD. This can be used for the student's portfolio, or taken home to share with family.

Presentation Skills Outside the Classroom

Many students already have experience creating movies and posting them online to sites such as YouTube without any guidance from teachers or parents, purely for entertainment value. Students generally use these videos to solicit comments and reactions by their friends. They may not have considered up until this point that these digital productions might become a permanent reflection of who they are.

> I suggest that teachers could make assignments that require students to publish their work on the Internet. Students would think much more critically before writing anything that was going to go into the digital sphere for the whole world to see. One of the wonderful things about the Internet today is its ability to solicit conversation. As students wrote and received comments from people all over the world it could encourage them to improve and write more.
>
> *Jeff VanDrimmelen, "Technology Should Be Used to Motivate Students," EDUCAUSE, http://tinyurl.com/9tufps*

Students are also publishing both personal work and schoolwork online in produced blogs that might offer scanned images of student-produced artwork and digital photographs, and sometimes publication of student research online. Blogs might be created independently by the student or as part of a class project. Either way, this process can help make students aware of the world of online publishing, preparing them for their future work where social networking sites and blogs will most likely be a natural part of how business is conducted.

When the time comes for the presentation of student curriculum-driven digital stories, the difference between personal entertainment and school-based projects could be part of the learning experience. Students will discover that it pays to consider who will be viewing their work and how it will be received.

Throughout the preparation and production stages, students should be encouraged to consider how the piece will be published or presented. A final peer review helps students fine-tune the 8- to 10-minute movie they will post to one of the video hosting sites listed in the following section.

> **Note:** Teachers should be attentive to what is being posted, as well as to what comments are being made. Student work ideally should be posted at student-oriented sites where there is some control over what is posted and the comments that follow.

Tools for Presenting Digital Stories Online

There are many websites for sharing and viewing student presentations and video curriculum material. There are also websites that allow users to upload files and create presentations online. Most of the examples presented here are free but require users to sign up and to have a password. Many have privacy options, and some have a fee option that allows for more storage space and an ad-free environment. Be sure to read the FAQs and the help files. Several have excellent tutorials and clearly written guidelines regarding the types of materials that may not be uploaded.

Video Hosting Sites

TeacherTube (www.teachertube.com) is a free video hosting website designed specifically for education and is the location of choice for student-created videos or digital stories. The file size limit is 100 MB, and presentations can be no longer than 10 minutes. Excellent directions plus uploaded videos can be downloaded if needed.

YouTube (www.youtube.com) is the widely known, free website that hosts a massive number of user-created videos with a wide range of purpose. This site is easy to use and features tutorial videos to help you get started with uploading. Users can upload as many as 10 videos at once, each with a maximum size of 1 GB. Teachers must closely monitor students' use of YouTube to avoid viewing of inappropriate content.

Presentation Creation Sites

Animoto (http://animoto.com) is a presentation creator that allows you to select a soundtrack when you upload your images, and the resulting combination is made into a video.

SlideRocket (www.sliderocket.com) is a free version of a presentation creator that is designed to be used completely online using your own digital images. You can upload existing presentations, then enhance and store them online.

SlideShare (www.slideshare.net) is a useful site for previously created presentations made in PowerPoint, Keynote, or Open Office formats, with a file size limit of 100 MB. Uploaded presentations can be shared or kept private. This site includes clearly written guidelines for use and is completely free.

LetterPop (http://letterpop.com) is a free online newsletter creator (10 free per year) allowing classrooms to create a printed (or e-mailed) newsletter to be sent home to parents promoting student digital stories. Simple newsletters are great for teaching students about marketing their work in a safe and controlled manner.

Resources

Presentation Skills and Marketing

Princeton University's McGraw Center—Oral Presentation Skills: http://web.princeton.edu/sites/mcgraw/oral_presentation_skills.html

Online Hosting

TeacherTube: www.teachertube.com

YouTube: www.youtube.com

Presentation Creators

Animoto: http://animoto.com

SlideRocket: www.sliderocket.com

SlideShare: www.slideshare.net

LetterPop: http://letterpop.com

Evaluating Digital Storytelling Projects

Designing the right kinds of assessment tools for curriculum-based digital storytelling projects should be tied to the curriculum requirements of your school district and of course the tenets of good writing. Both state and national guidelines are available to help you design assessments and meet benchmarks in curricular goals.

Note: Curriculum content standards and assessments should be applied in addition to specific assessment tools for digital storytelling.

Successful assessment begins with a well-developed lesson that includes a clearly defined assignment. It may appear that digital storytelling has a lot of gray areas because of the many ways in which a story can be told. Sometimes digital storytelling projects begin with a single-subject teacher, who assigns the story, then passes the creation and presentation steps to the instructor in the computer lab or library media center. These situations are more commonplace in schools with teamed learning goals. Lessons should be developed in partnership and may need to be approved by an administrator.

Formative assessment begins with the development of the assignment (see Chapter 2). Each student or each team of students should be informally assessed to determine whether they understand the process and goal of the assignment. Teachers may need to prepare a handout or put the assignment of the story's intent and purpose (with timeframe) on the class website for reference during the length of the project. As the project progresses, teachers, acting a mentors, can guide students effectively with the formative assessment tool as suggested in the following pages.

As outlined in Chapter 2, I suggest that teachers divide the digital storytelling project into stages, then break them down further into segments. I suggest further that each segment and each stage be assessed separately. Assessment rubrics help students understand how their grade will be determined, and most school districts have scoring or grading rubrics guidelines in place for teachers to adapt.

The online paper "Designing Scoring Rubrics for Your Classroom," by Craig A. Mertler of Bowling Green State University (http://pareonline.net/getvn.asp?v=7&n=25), presents several options for converting rubric scores to numerical grades and will help teachers who must use numerical grading methods. Jon Mueller's online "Authentic Assessment Toolbox" (http://jonathan.mueller.faculty.noctrl.edu/toolbox/rubrics.htm) is a must-read for definitions of holistic as compared to analytic rubrics.

I also recommend reviewing Edutopia's "Assessment Instructional Module" (www.edutopia.org/teaching-module-assessment/).

Creating Rubrics

The levels of mastery, or headings, in a formative rubric should be consistently labeled and clearly understood by students at the time the digital storytelling project is assigned. The WebQuest rubric (http://webquest.sdsu.edu/webquestrubric.html) suggests the following headings: beginning, developing, accomplished, and exemplary. These concepts are understandable for middle school and high school students. Individual digital storytelling projects need not include the exemplary heading because it is more appropriate for small-group projects within a whole class to increase the incentive for excellence and competition.

Each rubric section needs a scoring range of numerals for grading; for the younger student, wording in student-friendly terms should be used. Examine other rubrics to see how they might best work with, or be adapted to, your project. Some teachers include a bullet point or checklist of specific goals that need to be met for each section of the rubric.

Each example rubric offered in this chapter has been designed for one of the three stages of digital storytelling: preparation, production, or presentation.

Preparation Assessment

Digital storytelling often focuses on story; therefore, story development and the processes of good writing should be reflected in this rubric.

NETS•S Alignment

1. **Creativity and Innovation**

   a. apply existing knowledge to generate new ideas, products, or processes

   b. create original works as a means of personal or group expression

Preparation Rubric			
	Beginning	**Developing**	**Accomplished**
Assignment Comprehension	Student is passive and disconnected from the assignment and needs one-on-one help to get started with the project	Student understands the assignment but seems hesitant and questions the teacher each step of the way	Student takes initiative and comprehends the assignment and seeks answers to questions from peers before asking the teacher
Contributes to Discussion	Student does not seem interested in the discussion	Student pays attention and contributes an occasional thought or idea	Student is engaged and contributes ideas and listens to the ideas of others
Story Idea (story map)	Student has few ideas what the story will be about	Student has ideas about the story but needs assistance	Student grasps the story topic and begins to develop it

Preparation Rubric (continued)

	Beginning	Developing	Accomplished
Story Development (timeline)	Student knows what planning tools are needed but has questions about their use	Student makes some use of planning tools but needs help with organizing ideas	Student uses planning tools effectively and uses them with the writing process
First Draft	Student begins a first draft, but struggles with writing and doesn't meet the deadline	Students writes a first draft, but needs help with the editing process	Student writes a good first draft, meets the deadline date, and is ready for editing
Story Editing	Student struggles with suggested edits made by teacher or works too slowly	Student works well with the suggested edits made by the teacher	Student revises first draft in a timely manner; edits all work within deadline
Second Draft	Student's first draft edits are accepted, but student struggles with suggested additions made by the teacher	Student's first draft edits are accepted; student works to finish the suggested additions as directed	Student's first draft edits are accepted; student works quickly to add in additional material
Tenets of Good Writing	Second draft still has writing to be completed and needs grammar and sequence help	Second draft is complete but barely meets deadline and still has grammar errors	Second draft complete and within deadline time and shows improved writing since the first draft
Final Draft	Student is not ready to move to the production stage and may be frustrated waiting for the technology part to start	Student is ready to move to the production stage on time and shows continued interest in digital storytelling	Work is complete and student has time to start the production phase early; student interest is still high

Production Assessment

NETS•S Alignment

2. **Communication and Collaboration**

   a. interact, collaborate, and publish with peers, experts, or others employing a variety of digital environments and media

3. **Research and Information Fluency**

   b. locate, organize, analyze, evaluate, synthesize, and ethically use information from a variety of sources and media

4. **Critical Thinking, Problem Solving, and Decision Making**

   b. plan and manage activities to develop a solution or complete a project

5. **Digital Citizenship**

   a. advocate and practice safe, legal, and responsible use of information and technology

6. **Technology Operations and Concepts**

   b. select and use applications effectively and productively

   c. troubleshoot systems and applications

   d. transfer current knowledge to learning of new technologies

Production Rubric			
	Beginning	Developing	Accomplished
Locating Multimedia Elements	Student selects multimedia elements, but doesn't record original location and has to locate the source over again	Student selects multimedia elements and records and understands this process so that work can move forward independent of the teacher	Student meticulously locates and records each multimedia element and is willing to help others stay on track
Evaluating and Citing Elements	Student is beginning to understand the evaluation process and can write some citations	Student takes time to check each element and feels confident evaluating and citing media with only a little help from the teacher	Student evaluates and cites each element correctly both in the project notes and in the finished story
Digital Citizenship	Student is just beginning to learn about being a good digital citizen	Student grasps the concepts of fair use, ethical online behavior, and respect for intellectual property	Student promotes proper digital citizenship in digital storytelling and applies it to other projects
Knowledge of Software	Student needs help learning the software and is not willing to learn from another student	Student is competent with the software, but is passively sharing his or her knowledge with other students	Student has mastered the software needed and shares that expertise with other students
Troubleshooting Hardware and Software Issues	Student seeks help from teacher without trying to solve the problem	Student seeks help other students but still needs guidance from the teacher	Student works individually and in a group to solve hardware and software issues

continued

Production Rubric (continued)			
	Beginning	Developing	Accomplished
Phase One (assembly)	Student's progress is slow and random without meeting goals	Student's work meets goals within timeframe	Student's work is ordered, cited, evaluated, and completed
Phase Two (editing)	Student doesn't see the importance of editing and making changes	Student edits work, but is unclear why it is needed	Student's work is quickly edited and meets goals and timeframe
Phase Three (completion)	Student is behind schedule and has to return to goal sheet frequently to stay on target	Student work is on schedule and goals are met	Student works efficiently and quickly, meeting both goals and deadlines
Deadline	Doesn't meet deadline	Meets deadline	Meets deadline ahead of schedule and helps other students if asked

Presentation Assessment

For the digital storytelling project whose audience is to be online, the teacher should monitor audience feedback via the comments section of the online medium.

NETS•S Alignment

2. **Communication and Collaboration**

   b. communicate information and ideas effectively to multiple audiences using a variety of media and formats

5. **Digital Citizenship**

   b. exhibit a positive attitude toward using technology that supports collaboration, learning, and productivity

Presentation Rubric			
	Beginning	Developing	Accomplished
Lesson/ Discussion on Presenting Led by Teacher (face-to-face)	Student grasps the concept of the importance of audience but is apprehensive about the process of presenting	Student grasps the concept of the importance of audience and asks questions about the process of presenting	Student grasps the concept of the importance of audience and meets the challenge of presenting with confidence
Introduction to Story (written or PowerPoint introduction)	Student did not prepare adequately for introduction	Student scripted introduction but the result needs further editing for content and length	Student created and delivered an introduction appropriate for the assignment
Appearance/ Confidence Level	Student has taken little time with appearance; student doesn't make eye contact with audience	Student appearance is appropriate; student delivers the introduction with some eye contact	Student appearance is appropriate; student delivers the introduction with good eye contact and with enthusiasm
Positive Criticism by Peer Audience	Student is not influenced by peer comments	Student listens to peer comments but doesn't take them seriously	Student listens intently to peer comments and makes revisions based on them with teacher guidance
Lesson/ Discussion on Presenting Led by Teacher (online)	Student ignores lesson and clearly plans to post online without permission	Student absorbs lesson on the appropriateness of posting work online	Student meets the tenets of the rules of posting work online and promotes discussion about this topic with other students

Resources

Authentic Assessment Toolbox:
http://jonathan.mueller.faculty.noctrl.edu/toolbox/rubrics.htm

David Warlick's Rubric Machine:
http://landmark-project.com/rubric_builder

Designing Scoring Rubrics for Your Classroom:
http://pareonline.net/getvn.asp?v=7&n=25

Digital Storytelling Rubric: www.umass.edu/wmwp/
DigitalStorytelling/Rubric Assessment.htm

DigiTales—Overview of Evaluating Projects:
www.digitales.us/evaluating

The Educational Uses of Digital Storytelling: Rubrics:
http://digitalstorytelling.coe.uh.edu/rubrics.html

Edutopia—Core Concept: Comprehensive Assessment:
www.edutopia.org/assessment

Edutopia—Teaching Module: Assessment:
www.edutopia.org/teaching-module-assessment

Helen Barrett's Digital Storytelling Research Design:
http://electronicportfolios.org/digistory/ResearchDesign.pdf

WebQuest—A Rubric for Evaluating WebQuests:
http://webquest.sdsu.edu/webquestrubric.html

WebQuest—Rubrics for Web Lessons:
http://webquest.sdsu.edu/rubrics/weblessons.htm

PART II

Applying Digital Storytelling

Now that you have been introduced to the process of planning, producing, and presenting digital stories, it's time to give more thought to what digital storytelling can do. The chapters in this section present a number of suggestions for types of digital stories that work well in classrooms. We'll also talk about digital storytelling as a bridge between the classroom and the community—and how that connection to the larger world can spark interest and excitement in your students.

Building Enthusiasm for Learning

For K–12 students, digital storytelling can add sparkle to difficult topics. It can stimulate questions that other approaches might not. It is an active, not passive, process that can produce an atmosphere of excited learning and is inherently appealing to students.

But beyond this, students (especially older students) respond to having an audience and to having a real-world purpose for their work: to inform, to advocate, to reach out into the community and the world. Digital storytelling offers them this potential.

The Power of Audience

The power of audience and the appeal of publishing online can foster a new level of enthusiasm for the learning process in K–12 students. In the past, only the teacher, classmates, or family provided audience for student work. Now, knowing the work may be public in some way, and that it will be archived in the form of a movie, students tend to be more concerned about the end product than they were with paper-and-pencil projects.

In his article "The Power of Audience," (www.ascd.org/publications/educational_leadership/nov08/vol66/num03/The_Power_of_Audience.aspx) school designer Steven Levy notes:

> When student work culminates in a genuine product for an authentic audience, it makes a world of difference. Writing teachers know about the power of audience. When you write an essay, you have to know who your audience will be so that you can adjust your message and style accordingly. Chorus and band directors know the power of audience. Why do students work so hard practicing the same passages over and over, week after week? Because the audience is coming for the concert!

Personal Connections

There are two points on which teachers of digital storytelling projects usually agree: quality counts and should, in part, be evaluated according to the tenets of good composition; and the subject of the story should be something that the student feels emotionally charged about or has a definite personal interest in exploring.

Today's news media provide an endless stream of visual topics for students to choose from. Students' lives are affected by a wide range of issues such as global warming, war, and disease—issues they have no control over but do feel strongly about, whether they feel an emotional connection to them, are intellectually interested, or both.

Digital storytelling offers these students a voice. Students can learn to convey their views effectively to a wider audience than is usually available to them. They can share information or urge action on real-world issues that affect their schools and communities.

Some of my colleagues have found that short periods of reflective journaling during the preparation process assist students in focusing and narrowing the subject of the digital story project, whether it will be produced individually, in small groups, or by the whole class. Whole-class projects have proven to work most effectively with single subject disciplines. Whole-class digital storytelling might also be part of problem-based learning where students work to understand open-ended world problems they feel strongly about. Some high school classes are participating in community service projects, and through these activities, students have found a natural fit for digital storytelling.

Visual Literacy and Scrapbook Stories

At first glance, it may seem unusual to think of digital storytelling within the realm of old-fashioned scrapbooking. Teachers have traditionally used scrapbooks as an art form or, in photography classes, to have students learn the basics of composition, layout, and self-expression. So how does digital technology improve on the hands-on process of scrapbooking?

Digital scrapbooking, sometimes called e-scrapbooking, adds depth to traditional scrapbooking in two ways: first by teaching the art of preservation, and second by providing an expanded venue for students to share their work.

Digital scrapbooking is yet another hands-on activity that helps inform visual literacy, finding meaning with images, for K–12 students. In the past, teaching from textbooks provided students with only two ways to learn: reading text and looking at pictures. Students were passive observers. Classroom teachers augmented textbook experiences with visual media such as the chalkboard, filmstrips, or 16-millimeter movies.

Digital scrapbooking can be combined with traditional scrapbooking, providing the student with opportunities for hands-on learning. Students first create physical scrapbooks using scanned and digital photographs. Then they might add hand-drawn embellishments or even three-dimensional items (such as buttons,

> Visual digital storytelling can also be created from scraps purposefully quilted together as pieces of information, thoughts, emotions, and memories.

pins, ribbons, or paper clips) glued on for special effects. These pages can then be digitally photographed and combined into a movie with photos of the scrapbook creators and narration of the scrapbook stories. No one way is the right way, because this is an art form as well as a hands-on learning activity.

e-Scrapbooking

Annette Lamb provides and array of e-scrapbooking resources at her website (http://escrapbooking.com). Her background as a librarian and media specialist helped her create this superbly organized portal to related pedagogy, focused questions, books in print, and links that can jump-start any educator's interest in scrapbooking. Lamb defines e-scrapbooks as "tools for reflecting on ideas and sharing perspectives." She suggests that the *e* stands not only for electronic but also for educational, experiential, engaging, and expression.

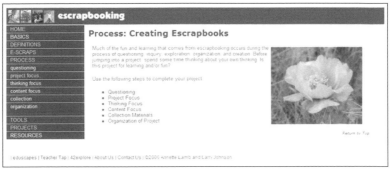

Annette Lamb's e-scrapbooking web pages

Working with primary sources is required by many states for standards-based learning lessons, projects, and activities. Lamb's activities offer ideas for using the American Memory collection from the Library of Congress (http://memory.loc.gov/ammem/) to create e-scrapbooks and digital stories, and for teaching visual literacy.

Scrapblog: Online Multimedia Scrapbooks

Alex de Carvalho and Carlos Garcia of Scrapblog (www. scrapblog.com) describe Scrapblog as "the first web-based service for creating and sharing multimedia scrapbooks online. It enables everyday people to express themselves online in creative ways. Users can aggregate their photos and videos from multiple online sources and mix them with audio, music, text, and thousands of creative elements in an environment that is truly drag-and-drop easy."

Scrapblog works well for classrooms because it's free and there is no online registration; therefore the Scrapblog service can be used by students at any computer, regardless of location. Students can create Scrapblogs in the classroom, computer lab, or library-media center and finish them as homework. Teachers can enhance the mentoring process by viewing the projects in progress in class and then quickly perform an assessment once students have published their Scrapblogs. Scrapblogs are also good story starters for larger projects.

I suggest teachers try making a three-slide Scrapblog themselves. If access is limited in the classroom, reserve time in the computer lab and work with the school technology facilitator, who may be able to teach the basics of using the Scrapblog Builder. Note that this is a browser-based tool, and any pop-up blocker should be disabled so that the Scrapblog Builder interface works in a separate window.

Scrapblog Builder, opening screen

Creating a Scrapblog

The following steps can be used to create a Scrapblog using the Scrapblog service.

1. After brainstorming story ideas, have students create a timeline in order to write a rough draft of the script. (See the Timelines section in Chapter 2.)

2. Then, students need to decide on the photo elements to include. Students can take their own pictures using a digital camera, scan and use an existing photo, or use photos copied from the web. Students also credit the sources of each photo or scan as part of this step. (This is a great opportunity to introduce an intellectual property lesson.)

3. Visual literacy lesson: Ask students several important critical thinking questions about the chosen photographs. Students then create and edit their rough draft based on discussions.

4. Students begin using Scrapblog to add their photos and/or scanned documents. If the resulting scrapbook pages are to be exported for printing in physical scrapbooks, the pages built should contain text to be read; if they are to be exported to be used in another application, such as Movie Maker, Photo Story, or iMovie, then the text should be only a visual clue for the vocal narration. Also important at this step is teaching good design and layout using backgrounds, stickers, shapes, and frames; students make the decision to use a theme or a blank page first.)

5. Scrapblogs should be saved frequently but should not be published until you have checked them with the prearranged assessment rubric.

6. There's an option for private or public viewing after publishing—only published Scrapblogs can be exported.

7. Exported Scrapblogs (JPEG format) can be sent to an existing photo-sharing account or to the computer's hard drive. You may wish to have students save their Scrapblogs to the computer so that the material is kept private.

8. Because the pages of the resulting Scrapblog are in a common format, they can be used as elements in movies, photo essays, or PowerPoint presentations. They can also become graphics for web pages.

9. Scrapblogs can be edited after they are published, but they must be exported again if changes were made to the pages.

Example Scrapblog page

A Sample Scrapblog: The Mariner and the Medal of Honor

Creating a Scrapblog and sharing it can an immensely rewarding experience. As an example, I created a Scrapblog: James A. Barber, Civil War Hero (www.scrapblog.com/ midgefrazel/476B3397-C8CA).

The U.S. Civil War is a great topic for a Scrapblog. Because photography was becoming more popular and common during the Civil War era, this war is the first so-called visual war: photographs began to tell the story of the conflict that both split and unified the United States. Many regional historical societies' photo collections contain photographs of local Civil War veterans returning home. There are also national collections of photographs, such as those by Mathew Brady, which capture amazing faces and terrible scenes of the battles.

Nearly every eastern U.S. city or town has memorials to this war with the names of those who served and an opportunity for students to record the names and learn about the people behind them. Local genealogy societies or veterans' organizations often have records of the location of veterans' graves, providing opportunities for students to visit and take photographs. Historians have created immense websites devoted to the details of the battles. These resources can make learning about this period of history engaging for students while providing a connection to local history. This way of preserving history is often called "Stories in Stone."

Links to several other examples of Scrapblogs are given in the Resources section at the end of this chapter.

ePortfolios

ePortfolios differ from regular digital stories in that they focus on the learning process, documenting the student's education experiences. ePortfolios may, for example, take the form of journals or photographic essays. Reflection and remembrance can make the process of creating an ePortfolio enjoyable. Creating an ePortfolio requires excellent planning, organizational, and archival skills. Making an ePortfolio is a dynamic way to show growth over time. Creating this type of digital story demonstrates that the student has mastered the curriculum goals and has the technological prowess to create, present, and store a project of this nature.

Having students respond to each other's ePortfolios is good practice for learning to give and receive constructive criticism and praise for a job well done. Sharing an ePortfolio with others who are just beginning can help them think clearly about the tasks and goals ahead and is a good mentoring experience for students.

Photo Essays

Photo essays are photograph collections that tell stories through this visual medium, with minimal or no text or narration. The story is in the pictures, and sometimes in the order of their presentation. Photo essays can be created with many software products.

A digital photo essay can be part of a digital story and can be part of an ePortfolio. Music tracks can be added to the product for added emphasis or to set the emotional tone. Photo essays are sometimes used to promote discussion in the classroom. The impact of an attractive presentation can elicit a strong emotional reaction from the audience.

Digital photo essays are sometimes used in the classroom to assist teachers—for example, to introduce the writing process in a poetry unit, or to teach students the steps of digital storytelling. In science classrooms, for example, it is important for students to understand the sequence of events in a life cycle. When presented with photographs of the stages of development, students demonstrate knowledge and understanding of growth and development by correctly sequencing photos. From this initial understanding can come critical thinking concerning what happens to an organism whose life cycle is interrupted or changed by the environment or predatory threats. By creating a photo essay, young students might begin to understand the scientific and mathematical concept "What comes next?" The possibilities are almost endless.

A Sample Photo Essay: Monarch Butterflies

Raising monarch butterflies in the classroom and taking digital photographs of each stage of development from egg to adult butterfly is a good hands-on, standards-based science lesson for elementary and middle school students.

Two excellent websites where you can find educational resources on the development and migration of monarch butterflies are Journey North—Monarch Butterflies (www.learner.org/jnorth/ tm/monarch/jr/KidsJourneyNorth.html) and Monarch Watch (www.monarchwatch.org).

The following figure is a one-page photo essay, in collage format, on monarch butterflies. Created with Scrapblog's School theme, the monarch butterfly collage was published as a Scrapblog, exported in JPEG format, sent to a Flickr account, and enhanced with a Museum border by using Picnik tools. This is an example of how, with just a few photos, a teacher could create a photo essay and use it to demonstrate a lesson or tell a story.

Monarch butterfly photo essay from author's collection

Resources

Annette Lamb's e-scrapbooking site: http://escrapbooking.com

eduScapes: http://eduscapes.com

Journey North—Monarch Butterflies:
www.learner.org/jnorth/monarch

Library of Congress American Memory collections:
http://memory.loc.gov/ammem

Monarch Watch: www.monarchwatch.org

Scrapblog: www.scrapblog.com

Examples of Scrapblogs

A Bit of Norway:
www.scrapblog.com/viewer/viewer.aspx?sbId=104630

Crossing into the Blue:
www.scrapblog.com/viewer/viewer.aspx?sbid=60174

James A. Barber, Civil War Hero:
www.scrapblog.com/midgefrazel/476B3397-C8CA

Journey to Rwanda:
www.scrapblog.com/viewer/viewer.aspx?sbId=140952

Digital Storytelling and Family History

Many students at all grades levels are interested in genealogy—the study of family history. This level of work may be beyond the scope of many classrooms. Still, I offer these thoughts and suggestions because you, the educator, may be able to adapt them to all kinds of class research projects. Moreover, you may have your own interest in genealogy—or discover one! I warn you, it's captivating and can be addictive.

Students often complain that the study of history is disconnected and meaningless to their lives. Learning about those who lived in the past and how they were connected to our families or our community can change the way students, regardless of ethnic background or cultural heritage, look at history. Exploring their own family history or local community history connects students to their past and almost always engages them. It can motivate them to share with others, to draw personal conclusions, and sometimes to dig deeper for more information.

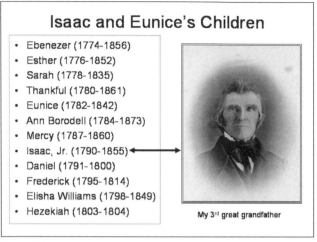

Isaac and Eunice's Children

- Ebenezer (1774-1856)
- Esther (1776-1852)
- Sarah (1778-1835)
- Thankful (1780-1861)
- Eunice (1782-1842)
- Ann Borodell (1784-1873)
- Mercy (1787-1860)
- Isaac, Jr. (1790-1855) ◄——————►
- Daniel (1791-1800)
- Frederick (1795-1814)
- Elisha Williams (1798-1849)
- Hezekiah (1803-1804)

My 3rd great grandfather

Ancestral photograph

Digital storytelling based on family or community history is one way we educators can inspire students to make learning about history a lifelong vocation. Motivation comes from the personalization and the hands-on nature of the work, and the fact that the end product can be shared with peers, family, and teachers.

Family historians and genealogists who make this work their life's vocation dig deeply into the past to find out who their grandparents, great-grandparents, and more remote ancestors were. They begin their search for answers to simple questions such as "Where were my ancestors born? Where did they live? Where did they die?"

This kind of search is likely to pique the curiosity of students at all grade levels. The questions and the topic have meaning and relevance in their own lives. Sadly, it's not always possible for students to research this kind of personal history in the confines of the classroom or the school.

Instead, students can practice this same kind of research on popular community leaders of the past. Almost every town and city has memorials to founders and heroes. The process could include having students take photographs, or search the Internet for photographs, of a city or state memorial or statue. As students research the person or persons memorialized, gather photographs, and write narrative text, a sense of identification and admiration for the community hero may grow.

Examining the lives of our presidents or of other famous figures, using information that is readily available on the Internet, can help students meet standards-based learning benchmarks while introducing them to the idea that their ancestors, too, have personal histories.

Research Questions

As students progress with an adapted lesson for a family history digital story project, I suggest questions similar to the following as a guide for their research:

- Who was this person (when born, married, and died)?

- What kind of work did this person/this family do?

- What heartaches or joys occurred in this family?

- Did the women in this family stay home and raise the children? Did all the children marry?

- When the children married or died, were they younger or older than the usual ages in families today?

- Were there issues of survival, periods of war, or economic situations that affected their lives?

- What do their gravestones tell you about their lives?

Family History Digital Story Ideas

Stories of Transitions: Arrivals and Departures

Relocation

People arrive in and depart from our lives with increasing frequency these days. For students whose lives have been disrupted when their family moved to another location, requiring them to change schools and friends, stories about places they have lived or places they dream about living may be the right ones for them to tell. Educators should expect students to have memories of sadness and joy and should look for this emotional aspect in their completed digital stories.

Immigration

There are many recorded oral histories and photographs of immigrants arriving and departing from Ellis Island in New York. Students can examine, analyze, and make meaningful reflections about these families. They might consider how the lives of these people were different before they left their homelands to come to the United States.

Thomas Edison filmed an early movie that can serve as an introduction to this type of project. I've collected some curriculum links on Ellis Island and immigration at Looking for America (www.midgefrazel.net/lookingforamerica.html).

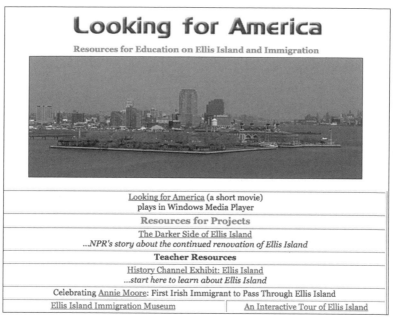

Looking for America

Resources for Education on Ellis Island and Immigration

Looking for America (a short movie) plays in Windows Media Player	
Resources for Projects	
The Darker Side of Ellis Island ...*NPR's story about the continued renovation of Ellis Island*	
Teacher Resources	
History Channel Exhibit: Ellis Island ...*start here to learn about Ellis Island*	
Celebrating Annie Moore: First Irish Immigrant to Pass Through Ellis Island	
Ellis Island Immigration Museum	An Interactive Tour of Ellis Island

Website with curriculum links on Ellis Island and immigration

Stories of Crossroads: Points of Intersection

Identifying points of intersection in our lives—critical events or moments that have significantly changed our lives—provides material for story content and opportunities for engaging in reflective writing. Examples of joys or tragedies might include moving to a new location, the births of younger siblings, earning academic or sports-related awards, or the death of a beloved grandparent or a childhood friend. Although there might not be photographs of these events, this type of digital story can be told in the first person as an audio podcast.

Examples of personal reflection stories can be found at the University of Houston's Educational Uses of Digital Storytelling site (http://digitalstorytelling.coe.uh.edu/personal_reflection. html) and at Creative Narrations (http://www.creativenarrations. net/site/storybook/).

Stories of Remembrance: Moments in Time

A single photograph in a family album can spark a conversation about who the people are, when the photograph was taken, and why that moment may have been chosen to snap the picture. Students may be surprised to discover that photography was a time consuming and expensive endeavor in the past, and that the process of taking, developing, and storing photographs was much different then.

Students are used to the immediacy of the digital image. Digital cameras have changed how we take photos and how we view the world in the viewfinder or LCD screen. Invite students to select a single image and write about it as if they were a journalist. Have a small group of students blend their images together into a "Moment in Time" story or photo essay.

Stories of Celebration and Culture: Tasty Memories

Many of us can be taken mentally to our grandmother's kitchen by a fleeting aroma of traditional family food. For many families, food is a rich part of the celebrations of life and is of cultural

Lasting Recipes digital story page

significance to us all. Stories can be told about family members who cooked special dishes at special times of the year. In many families, treasured recipes are passed down through generations.

Students can create digital stories about these legendary family cooks, or the dishes they prepared. Students can also research these foods and prepare a digital story answering questions such as, "What part of the world did this recipe come from?" and "How is my family's version of the recipe different from the traditional dish?"

Note: The Library of Congress is digitizing cookbooks of the past for students to peruse. An example is *A First American Cookbook* (www. loc.gov/exhibits/treasures/tri054.html). Another cookbook project can be found at *Feeding America* (http://digital.lib.msu.edu/projects/ cookbooks/).

More Research Questions for Digital Stories and Family History

- What does your story tell us about your home life?

- What would your family be like if they lived in another era?

- What other person in your family do you feel you are most like (physically or emotionally)?

- If you had the chance to meet one of your ancestors, which one would it be and why?

Resources

Creative Narrations—Digital Storybook (more personal reflection stories): www.creativenarrations.net/site/storybook/

Educational Uses of Digital Storytelling—Personal reflection stories: http://digitalstorytelling.coe.uh.edu/personal_reflection.html

Feeding America: http://digital.lib.msu.edu/projects/cookbooks/

A First American Cookbook: www.loc.gov/exhibits/treasures/tri054.html

Looking for America: www.midgefrazel.net/lookingforamerica.html

Digital Storytelling: A Bridge to the Community

At the beginning of the 20th century, education in the U.S. prepared students for the agricultural and factory workplace. Many community schools graduated their last farmers by the end of the 1930s or early 1940s. During the 1950s and 1960s, students were made ready for jobs in an industrialized society. Today's students will enter a different workplace than their parents did—a workplace that deals in information as much as in goods and services, and whose marketplace is the Internet. They will enter not a national society, but a global one.

Keeping the classroom in touch with the world outside has always been challenging for educators. The emergence of the Internet has let the classroom expand with greater ease beyond its walls and into the community. And that community has become a global community that is increasingly reflected in the classroom. Students are more diverse than ever in their places of birth, languages, and cultures.

As students prepare for their future, they must learn about other places and different cultures. They must learn how to relate to people who live and work in those places. The Internet has narrowed the distance between classrooms, bringing them together from around the globe. "Digital storytelling in the community" may mean the local community, the national community, or even a community on another continent.

Beyond the Classroom Walls

Global collaboration at the middle and high school level can yield some terrific learning experiences with the ever-expanding access to photographs, videos, and music that the Internet can provide. Stories of places both near and far are being created, transformed into video, and shared by K–12 students. Younger students are eager to learn about the neighborhood around their school, but as students get older, this neighborhood can extend, via the Internet, beyond their town, city, state, or country.

Curriculum areas in social studies, such as geography and local history, are a natural fit for digital storytelling in the local community, bridging classroom to community. Students benefit from the experience of exploring the world around their school with the help of a digital or video camera. Researching local heroes, both past and present, can result in digital stories rich with oral history interviews, displays created for local museums and libraries, and presentations given to community groups.

Community-based science projects can foster awareness of local community issues such as recycling, conservation, and beautification of community property. These projects can help students build a memorable and lifelong connection to their community.

National or global issues such as global warming, medical care, nutrition, and dependency on fossil fuels are a few examples of current issues students can learn more about through research and digital storytelling. And such projects can be a way for students to feel actively involved in issues they care about. Every teacher can remember at least one bored and apathetic student who became engaged and enthusiastic through making hands-on discoveries, and then sharing those discoveries with teachers and peers.

Opportunities for connection to the community through curriculum-based projects in digital storytelling could involve, for example, developing mapping skills, learning about GPS technology, studying local community laws, or exploring geophysical concepts. Applying lessons learned in the classroom to community outreach projects often helps bring learning to life for students in all grade levels.

Digital Storytelling Ideas for History, Science, and Community Issues

- Community-based projects
- Restoration of local parks
- Study of local memorials
- Study of local architecture
- Local heroes
- Investigation of local rivers, ponds, and other waterways
- Local landscaping projects
- Neighborhood service helpers (fire, police, medical)
- Restoration of local historical graveyards
- Importance of affordable housing

Place-Based Digital Storytelling

Making a connection between past and present is a concept that some students struggle with and others find intriguing. Here are just a few thoughts that can stimulate a classroom discussion: Think of your own home, school, or neighborhood as it looks today. Do you know how was it different in the past? Can you imagine what it looked like? The notions that streets were originally dirt paths, didn't have sidewalks, or even had a different name are the kinds of ideas that might stimulate students' imagination and a lively discussion.

An interesting related topic is that maps on paper are different from online and GPS-created maps. Some students may wonder how people managed to navigate without GPS, or at least an online map that gives driving directions. Others may be eager to share that their family still keeps paper maps in the glovebox and gets around just fine.

Place-based digital storytelling, often called storymapping, is a form of digital storytelling that uses online mapping tools such as Google Maps (http://maps.google.com) or CommunityWalk (www.communitywalk.com). Students choose a familiar area nearby, or one they have previously visited (for example, on a class fieldtrip), find it with the mapping tool, and create a digital story in narrative form. Students place photos on the map, and the story develops from the actual place.

Brenda Dyck has created a model of this mashup of mapping and digital storytelling on her website: Find a Story . . . Map a Story . . . Tell a Story (www.rebooting.ca/place/). Her project idea is to have students locate a map of a memorable area, one they can tell a story about. Students place markers on the map corresponding to parts of the story. On Brenda's site, she offers several examples of this combination of story and place as a digital experience, as well as step-by-step instructions for lesson building and a suggested rubric.

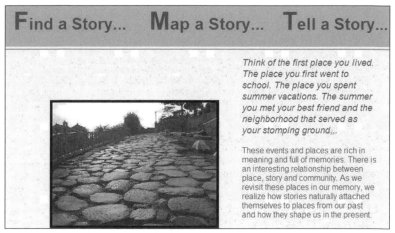

Brenda Dyck's place-based storytelling web page

Annette Lamb and her husband Larry Johnson have created a resource that builds on the place-based storytelling concept, enhancing the learning experience through the use of GPS devices (http://eduscapes.com/omrp/gps.htm). The GPS and GIS technology brings virtual nature walks, or virtual walks through history, into classrooms that may be far from such places. Students who live in the city can now experience the stories in literature where nature is a theme, or "visit" important locations from their history books. Extended to global classroom partnerships, this approach may become a new, collaborative way to look at geography.

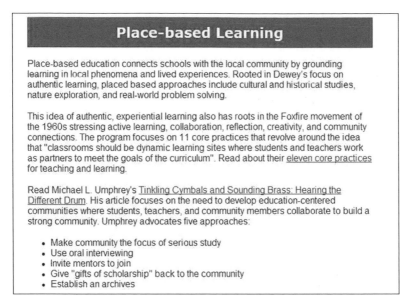

Place-based Learning

Place-based education connects schools with the local community by grounding learning in local phenomena and lived experiences. Rooted in Dewey's focus on authentic learning, placed based approaches include cultural and historical studies, nature exploration, and real-world problem solving.

This idea of authentic, experiential learning also has roots in the Foxfire movement of the 1960s stressing active learning, collaboration, reflection, creativity, and community connections. The program focuses on 11 core practices that revolve around the idea that "classrooms should be dynamic learning sites where students and teachers work as partners to meet the goals of the curriculum". Read about their eleven core practices for teaching and learning.

Read Michael L. Umphrey's Tinkling Cymbals and Sounding Brass: Hearing the Different Drum. His article focuses on the need to develop education-centered communities where students, teachers, and community members collaborate to build a strong community. Umphrey advocates five approaches:

- Make community the focus of serious study
- Use oral interviewing
- Invite mentors to join
- Give "gifts of scholarship" back to the community
- Establish an archives

Annette Lamb's place-based story web page

Cultural Digital Storytelling

In every community, and to some extent at every grade level, students learn about cultures near and far. Whether it is a standards-based activity meant to prepare students for test-taking, or a supplement to other core-curriculum studies and activities, student research into domestic or foreign cultures is now supported by a growing collection of online resources that can be applied in the students' digital stories.

Rushton Hurley, founder of Next Vista for Learning (www.nextvista.org), has created an online repository for educational videos created by teachers and students. His website hosts a growing variety of curriculum-based short videos. Hurley also promotes digital storytelling in his presentations to educators at local and national conferences, encouraging teachers to work with the wide variety of video-making applications to create their own curriculum-based videos.

In his Light Bulbs collection, Hurley has created a video, *Introduction to Japanese Religion*, for high school students and their teachers as a basis for understanding how religion and culture are strongly intertwined in the everyday life of the Japanese people. This video could be used as an example of how students might create stories that introduce globally significant topics to their fellow classmates.

Next Vista for Learning web page

Hurley has provided a way for educators to download the video for offline use in the classroom (see figure above). Because many of the other video-hosting web portals are often blocked by schools' content filtering, it is important for educators to be able to freely download videos for offline viewing. The comments section of Next Vista provides a way for educators to share how they used these videos in their teaching.

Scientific Digital Storytelling

Students who are inspired by the wonder of nature and possess natural curiosity about the scientific world will find their own level of emotional connection to tell the stories of their future plans for invention, medicine, and even saving our planet.

Weather, especially extreme weather, is a fascinating science topic for many students. Storm science can tell us about the history of our Earth, and it can also provide great material for digital storytelling. Natural disasters and the events following them provide stories about storms and the science behind them, and also about the people these storms affect. After a storm has ripped a community apart, stories about character, teamwork, and community rebuilding are there to be told.

A project of this scope—and this is only one small idea—requires fact-based evidence research and oral interviews. It also requires a certain amount of imagination and creativity on the part of the student. Often, it's these kinds of challenges that engage and motivate students who might otherwise have stayed slumped at their desks.

Expanding on the ideas of using storm science as the basis of a digital story project, students could visit their local library or historical society to look for photos of the effects of extreme weather in their own city or town. Conducting research in this way helps students learn valuable archival and research skills.

Also, local historians can be the voice telling the stories of wintry blizzards, wild tornadoes, or hurricane devastation, and how the community was rebuilt. Related stories might focus on the prediction of ferocious storms, or on how people survive them when they come. For example, New Englanders are fiercely proud of stories of powerful hurricanes, humid summer heat, and springtime blizzards. These stories have been passed down orally, some for generations. Digital storytelling offers another way to preserve such stories. Every community and family has photographs and yarns to spin around the storm of such and such a year.

Links to some good websites to search for photos of wild weather can be found in the Resources section at the end of this chapter.

Wild weather example photograph

Global Digital Storytelling

Students have a natural curiosity about the daily lives and experiences of their peers in distant parts of the globe. If children are starving or soldiers are dying, students often feel an emotional connection to those unseen faces in unseen places. Questions of global community are important in the lives of today's students, perhaps more so than in previous generations. When seeking out a subject for this area of digital storytelling, I suggest that you take a broad view of today's world issues. Perhaps begin by posing a question to your students about one of these issues or about an interesting area of the world. (Of course, this work must fit with your curriculum content and should be assessed on that basis.)

The Internet makes collaboration between classrooms possible, even when those classrooms are on opposite sides of the globe. Although there are always issues when conducting multiclassroom projects, digital storytelling can make the process more practical. Because an online digital story can be presented asynchronously, time zone differences are minimized. Additionally, digital stories, especially formats that rely primarily or exclusively on images and video, can help bridge language barriers.

Examples of these types of stories can be found at the Next Vista for Learning website (www.nextvista.org), which includes Global Views, a collection of videos about communities around the world that were made by and for teenagers.

Open-Ended Questions: Digital Storytelling and Community

These sample open-ended questions are provided to give you, the educator, ideas for developing critical thinking activities to accompany digital storytelling projects. They are meant as samples, and I encourage you to make up your own that may best fit your curriculum and your project. Consider the timeline for each phase of the project and how the digital story will be told before deciding on the guiding question.

* What is the best way to decide whether a particular photo has historical significance?

* What questions might future generations have about the digital stories we tell today?

* What ideas do you have on how technology assists teachers, parents, and students to learn more about local and global geography as part of a better understanding of the global economy?

Resources

Historical and Cultural

Flickr—The Commons (publicly-held photography collections): www.flickr.com/commons

Library of Congress Photos on Flickr: Frequently Asked Questions: www.loc.gov/rr/print/flickr_pilot_faq.html

My Friend Flickr: A Match Made in Photo Heaven: www.loc.gov/blog/?p=233

Next Vista for Learning: www.nextvista.org

Place-Based, or StoryMapping

Find a Story... Map a Story... Tell a Story...: www.rebooting.ca/place/

GPS and Place-Based Learning (Annette Lamb): http://eduscapes.com/omrp/gps.htm

CommunityWalk: www.communitywalk.com

Google Maps: http://maps.google.com

Weather

Wild Weather, NOAA Weather Library: www.photolib.noaa.gov

Creative Commons: Search for Images: http://search.creativecommons.org

Weather Links at Kathy Schrock's Guide for Educators: http://school.discoveryeducation.com/schrockguide/weather.html

A Final Word about Digital Storytelling

We've used the phrase *digital storytelling* in this book to cover a broad array of projects and products, including scrapbooks, portfolios, class research projects, and independent research projects. The digital tools available on the Internet as part of the Web 2.0 family of open-source software have opened up a whole new world for the application of hands-on learning in the K–12 classroom.

Classic digital storytelling applies the tools we have reviewed in this book to bring classic storytelling, the written or oral presentation of story, to life on the computer screen, shared with the audience through further application of the technologies.

It is my firm hope that you will find the right application for these tools in your classroom.

Digital Storytelling for Educators

This appendix is for educators seeking to learn more about how the technology of digital storytelling might help them professionally. It is also for teacher educators seeking resources for the university classroom or to employ in professional development workshops. Educators seeking acceptance into doctoral programs now often submit digital portfolios (or ePortfolios), another genre of digital storytelling.

Promoting Digital Storytelling in Higher Education

In the past ten years, higher education in the United States has made a concerted effort to update and upgrade teacher education courses to meet the demands of emerging and evolving educational technology tools.

Example—Tapped In chat

technology at Concordia University in Portland, Oregon, also runs her own consulting business. She understands the power of ePortfolios and is the owner of the ePortfolio group at Tapped In. As an online host, she encourages the exchange of ideas on ePortfolio standards, purposes, and goals by inviting others who have created ePortfolios as guest moderators.

ePortfolios for Educators

It is common practice for undergraduate students in teacher education programs to begin a portfolio of their learning experiences in higher education and add to it through their student teaching semester. In the past, these portfolios were paper-based scrapbooks of best practice lessons, class reflections, and photographs, demonstrating the story of students' preservice teaching and learning experiences. In educational technology classes, both graduate and undergraduate students began adding digital elements (videos, digital images, and audio) to their autobiographies. These new ideas made it possible to add more dimensions to the stories of their experiences and successes. With online hosting of these portfolios, students expanded their audience and suddenly had greater ease in sharing their background with potential employers, or as part of graduate school applications.

Because of controversy involving intellectual property ownership rights for materials used in ePortfolios, students creating them learn firsthand the importance of citing sources of digital elements. This experience provides a valuable background for their future professional work. For the university instructor, the assignment of the ePortfolio should be clearly presented, with guidelines for production and assessment. The process should include instruction in the same types of techniques future educators will provide their own students, including screen-capture techniques, proper citation methods, and permission gathering as a way of building on the professional experience.

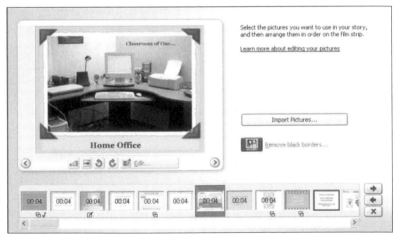

Example of an ePortfolio in Photo Story

Helen Barrett, an educational consultant researching emerging strategies for electronic portfolios and digital storytelling, has assembled a comprehensive online resource for educators building and teaching ePortfolios. In her blog e-Portfolios for Learning (http://electronicportfolios.com/blog/), Barrett writes about the ePortfolio as story. She suggests that because the portfolio requirement of many colleges and universities has become a sort of test, the idea of audience for this important reflective story tool has been transformed. I suggest visiting her blog, where you'll find a wealth of information on the ePortfolio.

Storytelling in the Age of the Internet

Gail Matthews-DeNatale, Associate Director of Academic Technology at Simmons College in Boston, Massachusetts, collaborates with faculty at Simmons and other area colleges and universities to prepare multimedia rich seminars and graduate courses. One of these, "Storytelling in the Age of the Internet," has been posted to the EDUCAUSE Resource Center (www.educause.edu/Resources/StorytellingintheAgeoftheInter/159755/) for sharing with other institutions of higher learning. In addition to an extensive list of digital storytelling websites and books, Matthews-DeNatale and her colleagues have posted their PowerPoint presentation, a sample digital story and two video clips. The presentation includes the basics of digital storytelling; information on storyboard, script, and timeline development; and suggestions for the order in which digital storytelling projects should be presented. The team at Simmons College deserves the attention of all educators for sharing these resources for those who are working with digital story making courses.

Open-Ended Questions: Digital Storytelling for Educators

These sample open-ended questions are provided to give teacher educators sample topics to use for discussion when developing digital storytelling lessons and projects.

- Teachers often expect that a class in digital storytelling should be about using the tools and not about the writing process. In your opinion, are teachers wrong to expect a step-by-step class in the use of this technology?

- Who owns the content of an ePortfolio or digital story?

- Is it important to assess the technological skills of students in the same rubric as the writing? How can teachers emphasize the writing when the students see the technology skills as more pertinent to their lives?

- Whose responsibility is it to teach the importance of digital citizenship? Should classroom teachers expect the technology facilitator to cover this in each grade?

Resources for Educators

Professional Development

Digital Storytelling: Examining the Process with Middle School Students (Stacy Behmer's resources for her graduate work at Iowa State University): http://ctlt.iastate.edu/~ds/Behmer

Digital Storytelling, Visual Literacy and 21st Century Skills article: www.techlearning.com/techlearning/pdf/events/techforum/ny05/Vault_article_jakesbrennan.pdf

Educational Technology and Life blog by Mark Wagner:
http://edtechlife.com

Integrating 21st Century Skills into the Curriculum (sample
course): http://docs.google.com/Doc?id=dd9szsgd_88hjhsnn

Read•Write•Think—Digital Reflections: Expressing Understanding
of Content through Photography (lesson for Grades 6–8):
www.readwritethink.org/lessons/lesson_view.asp?id=985

21st Century Skills for Teachers: A Graduate Level Class blog post:
http://edtechlife.com/?p=1915

Tapped In

Tapped In: www.tappedin.org

Tapped In Calendar:
http://tappedin.org/tappedin/do/CalendarAction

Digital Storytelling The War: The Power of Story:
www.pbs.org/thewar/edu_power_of_story.htm

ePortfolio

Electronicportfolios.org (Helen's Barrett's resources for electronic
portfolios): http://electronicportfolios.org

E-Portfolios for Learning: http://electronicportfolios.org/blog

Campus Technology—*The ePortfolio Hijacked* by Trent Batson:
www.campustechnology.com/ articles/2007/12/the-eportfolio-
hijacked.aspx

Author's ePortfolio at YouTube:
www.youtube.com/watch?v=juckzpNQ8lc

National Educational Technology Standards for Students (NET•S)

All K–12 students should be prepared to meet the following standards and performance indicators.

1. **Creativity and Innovation**
   Students demonstrate creative thinking, construct knowledge, and develop innovative products and processes using technology. Students:

   a. apply existing knowledge to generate new ideas, products, or processes

   b. create original works as a means of personal or group expression

   c. use models and simulations to explore complex systems and issues

   d. identify trends and forecast possibilities

2. **Communication and Collaboration**
   Students use digital media and environments to communicate and work collaboratively, including at a distance, to support individual learning and contribute to the learning of others. Students:

   a. interact, collaborate, and publish with peers, experts, or others employing a variety of digital environments and media

   b. communicate information and ideas effectively to multiple audiences using a variety of media and formats

   c. develop cultural understanding and global awareness by engaging with learners of other cultures

   d. contribute to project teams to produce original works or solve problems

3. **Research and Information Fluency**
   Students apply digital tools to gather, evaluate, and use information. Students:

   a. plan strategies to guide inquiry

   b. locate, organize, analyze, evaluate, synthesize, and ethically use information from a variety of sources and media

   c. evaluate and select information sources and digital tools based on the appropriateness to specific tasks

   d. process data and report results

4. **Critical Thinking, Problem Solving, and Decision Making**
   Students use critical-thinking skills to plan and conduct research, manage projects, solve problems, and make informed decisions using appropriate digital tools and resources. Students:

   a. identify and define authentic problems and significant questions for investigation

   b. plan and manage activities to develop a solution or complete a project

   c. collect and analyze data to identify solutions and make informed decisions

   d. use multiple processes and diverse perspectives to explore alternative solutions

5. **Digital Citizenship**
   Students understand human, cultural, and societal issues related to technology and practice legal and ethical behavior. Students:

   a. advocate and practice the safe, legal, and responsible use of information and technology

   b. exhibit a positive attitude toward using technology that supports collaboration, learning, and productivity

   c. demonstrate personal responsibility for lifelong learning

   d. exhibit leadership for digital citizenship

6. **Technology Operations and Concepts**
Students demonstrate a sound understanding of technology concepts, systems, and operations. Students:

a. understand and use technology systems

b. select and use applications effectively and productively

c. troubleshoot systems and applications

d. transfer current knowledge to the learning of new technologies

Image Credits

Page 16: © 2007–2008 Carole McCulloch; Digital Storytelling Network, Australia. Screenshot and photographs used with permission.

Page 44: © 2007–2008 Microsoft Corporation. All rights reserved. PowerPoint is a trademark of Microsoft Corporation.

Page 46: © 2007–2008 Google. All rights reserved.

Page 52: © 2007–2008 Flickr and the Library of Congress "The Commons." "Sylvia Sweets Tea Room, Brockton, MA," no known copyright restrictions. www.flickr.com/photos/library_of_congress/2178249475

Page 55: © 2007–2008 Melinda Kolk, Tech4Learning.com. Twist and the Twist logo are trademarks of Tech4Learning.com. Screenshot used with permission.

Pages 63–65: iMovie '08 screenshots © 2007–2008 Apple, Inc. All rights reserved.

Pages 63–65: © 2008 Kathleen Schrock. Photographs and screenshots used with permission by Kathy Schrock.

Page 66: © 2008 Tony Vincent. Screenshot and storyboard used with permission from learninginhand.com.

Pages 69–81: Photo Story 3 and Movie Maker 2 screenshots © 2007–2008 Microsoft Corp. All rights reserved.

Page 84: © 2007–2008 Audacity. All rights reserved. Public domain music from Musopen.org: Piano Sonata No. 14 in C-sharp minor by Ludwig van Beethoven.

Page 113: © 2008 Annette Lamb. Screenshots used with permission from Eduscapes.com, Annette Lamb, and Larry Johnson.

Pages 115, 117: © 2007–2008 Alex DeCarvahlo and Carols Garcia, Scrapblog.com. Screenshots used with permission. Scrapblog.com is the first online multimedia scrapbooking site.

Page 135: © 2008 Brenda Dyck, University of Alberta (Edmonton, Canada).

Page 136: © 2008 Annette Lamb. Screenshots used with permission from Eduscapes.com, Annette Lamb, and Larry Johnson.

Page 137: © 2007–2008 Rushton Hurley, Next Vista for Learning. Screenshot used with permission from digital storytelling movie at nextvista.org.

Page 147: © 2007–2008 Patricia Byers, SRI International. Screenshot used with permission, Tapped In is owned and operated by SRI International.